Taiwan

Taiwan

BY DAVID C. KING

Enchantment of the World
Second Series

Children's Press®

A Division of Scholastic Inc.

NEW YORK   TORONTO   LONDON   AUCKLAND   SYDNEY
MEXICO CITY   NEW DELHI   HONG KONG
DANBURY, CONNECTICUT

Frontispiece: Tienhsiang Pagoda is a popular tourist destination in the Taroko Gorge.

Consultant: Murray Rubinstein, PhD, Department of History, Baruch College,
The City University of New York

Please note: All statistics are as up-to-date as possible at the time of publication.

Book production by Herman Adler Design

Library of Congress Cataloging-in-Publication Data

King, David C.
  Taiwan / by David C. King.
    p. cm. — (Enchantment of the world. Second series)
  Published simultaneously in Canada.
  Audience: Ages 10–14.
  Audience: Grades 7–8.
  Includes index.
  ISBN 0-516-24856-1
  1. Taiwan—Juvenile literature. I. Title. II. Series.
  DS799.K58 2006
  951.24'9—dc22   2005021743

CHILDREN'S PRESS and associated logos are trademarks and/or registered
trademarks of Scholastic Library Publishing. SCHOLASTIC and associated logos
are trademarks and/or registered trademarks of Scholastic Inc.
1 2 3 4 5 6 7 8 9 10 R 15 14 13 12 11 10 09 08 07 06

Taiwan

Contents

Cover photo:
A pagoda

Rice field

Qing Dynasty vase

Province or Country?

THE ISLAND OF TAIWAN IS A COMBINATION OF FAST-PACED urban life and serene natural beauty. Modern cities with towering skyscrapers and traffic-clogged streets are only a few miles from rugged mountains with crystal-clear lakes and lush plant life.

Modern, urban Taiwan has emerged with startling speed. As recently as 1950, the island was a quiet agricultural backwater. By the 1960s, farm villages were giving way to booming factory towns and Taiwan was becoming an industrial

Opposite: **Kaoshiung is a modern city filled with tall buildings and crowded streets.**

A craftworker makes a saxophone in Houli. Taiwan is one of the world's leading exporters of saxophones.

The citizens of Taiwan are proud of their country. These children work hard to clean up a playground.

powerhouse. But Taiwan's "economic miracle" brought new problems. Industries that produced steel, trucks, ships, and other goods also produced deadly pollution. Within a decade, pollution was destroying plant and animal life, making waterways filthy, and forcing city dwellers to wear surgical masks as protection against the smog.

The Taiwanese people have attacked these problems with incredible energy and creativity. Industries that generate a lot of pollution are being replaced by cleaner industries, such as those that produce components for computers and other high-technology products. The government has also addressed the pollution problem by building a high-speed rapid transit system and encouraging motorists to use cleaner fuel. Schools today provide environmental education at all grade levels, and private organizations sponsor weekend cleanup campaigns in parks and on hiking trails. Roughly 20 percent of the island is now protected and divided into parks and nature reserves.

In the Shadow of a Giant

The Taiwanese also face a more abstract problem: the problem of identity. The island lies in the shadow of mainland China, the world's most populous nation and one of the most powerful. To the government and people of mainland China—officially called the People's Republic of China—Taiwan is a province. Some Taiwanese agree. After all, more than 95 percent of the island's people are of Chinese descent. And the culture and history of the island emerge from the culture and history of the mainland.

But many Taiwanese do not believe that Taiwan is a province. They view their island as a separate entity, one that is wealthier and more democratic than the mainland and that is rapidly creating its own culture. There is a strong belief among many Taiwanese that Taiwan should be considered a nation. A very small number of Taiwanese cling to the belief that Taiwan is the

Most of Taiwan's citizens are of Chinese descent.

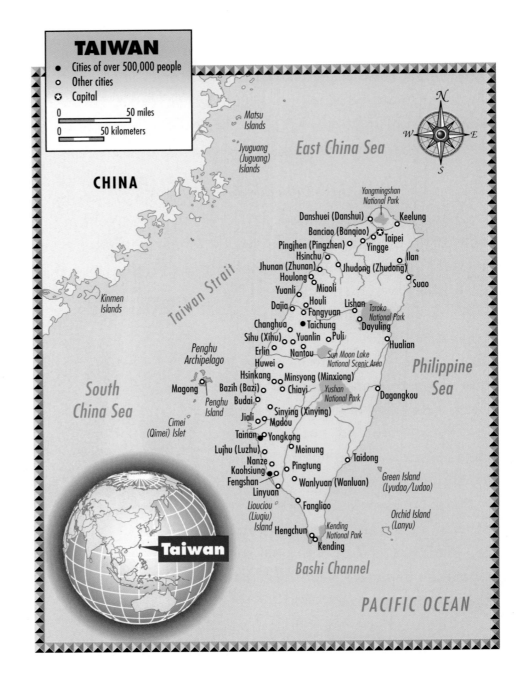

TAIWAN

- ● Cities of over 500,000 people
- ○ Other cities
- ✪ Capital

0   50 miles

0   50 kilometers

CHINA

East China Sea

Matsu Islands

Jyuguang (Juguang) Islands

Taiwan Strait

Kinmen Islands

Penghu Archipelago

Magong

Penghu Island

Cimei (Qimei) Islet

South China Sea

Danshuei (Danshui)
Banciao (Banqiao)
Pingjhen (Pingzhen)
Hsinchu
Jhunan (Zhunan)
Houlong
Yuanli
Dajia
Changhua
Sihu (Xihu)
Erlin
Huwei
Hsinkang
Bazih (Bazi)
Budai
Jiali
Madou
Tainan
Lujhu (Luzhu)
Nanze
Kaohsiung
Fengshan
Linyuan
Liouciou (Liuqiu) Island

Yangmingshan National Park
Keelung
Taipei
Yingge
Ilan
Jhudong (Zhudong)
Miaoli
Suao
Houli
Lishan
Taroko National Park
Fongyuan
Taichung
Yuanlin
Puli
Dayuling
Nantou
Sun Moon Lake National Scenic Area
Hualian
Minsyong (Minxiong)
Chiayi
Yushan National Park
Dagangkou
Sinying (Xinying)
Yongkang
Meinung
Pingtung
Taidong
Wanlyuan (Wanluan)
Green Island (Lyudao/Ludao)
Fangliao
Orchid Island (Lanyu)
Hengchun
Kending National Park
Kending

Philippine Sea

Bashi Channel

PACIFIC OCEAN

Taiwan

"true China" and that it will someday take the lead in creating a unified and democratic China.

General Chiang Kai-shek and his Nationalist government fled China for Taiwan in 1949.

The people of Taiwan have wrestled with this issue for more than fifty years. During that time, they have lived with the uncertainty of what that giant on their doorstep intends to do. After all, how could an island of nearly 23 million people defend itself against a nation of well over one billion?

Complicated Conflict

The conflict between the island and the mainland is a complicated and sometimes confusing story, even to the Taiwanese. In 1949, Communists gained control of mainland China. Communists believe that a nation's government should control all aspects of the economy and own all businesses. When the Communists ousted the Nationalist government, headed by Chiang Kai-shek, the Nationalist leadership fled to Taiwan. Chiang's Nationalists, officially called the Kuomintang (or KMT), established a firm dictatorship on the island, ruthlessly crushing all opposition. Chiang insisted that the Nationalists would soon invade the mainland and reunite the country. This dream was never fulfilled, and today only a handful of Taiwanese still believe the two can be reunited.

For its part, the People's Republic of China (PRC) has kept its coastline well-armed. From time to time, the PRC has shelled offshore islands occupied by Taiwan. Mainland China has also tried to intimidate the Taiwanese, especially during elections, by firing "test" missiles that have landed within a few miles of Taiwan itself.

Taiwan televises war games each year to assure the public that the government is prepared in case China attacks.

The people of Taiwan have lived with this insecurity for more than fifty years. During that time, they also put up with the harsh rule of the KMT government, largely because its policies of building industry and trade fueled Taiwan's staggering economic growth. Within twenty years, the island developed one of the most successful economies in all of Asia. Four decades of KMT dictatorship ended after the death of Chiang Kai-shek in 1975 and of his son a decade later. Today, Taiwan has developed a democratic government.

The conflict with the mainland remains unsettled. Beijing is the capital of the People's Republic of China; Taipei is the capital of Taiwan. The Beijing government insists on a policy of "one country, two systems." That is, they want the Taiwanese to accept that there is just one country—China—and that Taiwan is one of its provinces. But China agrees that the island can have its own system for managing Taiwanese affairs. Talks to see if some compromise can be reached have occasionally been held. Many Taiwanese feel that it's time to declare independence, but the Taipei government has been more cautious, and there has been no outright statement of independence.

Most Taiwanese do not seem to feel that they are in real danger of being overwhelmed by their huge and powerful neighbor. As one Taipei businessman pointed out, "We have lived with that danger for nearly sixty years. In that time we have become larger, stronger, more prosperous, and more democratic. I think the Chinese hope to become more like us, rather than the other way 'round."

"Beautiful Island"

TAIWAN IS LOCATED JUST 80 MILES (130 KILOMETERS) OFF the coast of China, separated from the mainland by the Taiwan Strait. It is part of an island chain that stretches along the entire east coast of Asia. Taiwan itself includes dozens of small islands divided into three groups, or archipelagos. From above, Taiwan has the shape of a leaf, or maybe a large sweet potato. It measures 245 miles (394 km) in length and 89.5 miles (144 km) at its widest point. It covers 14,015 square miles (36,300 sq km), slightly larger than the combined area of Maryland and Delaware, but its population of nearly 23 million makes it one of the most crowded places on earth.

The bodies of water surrounding Taiwan are all parts of the Pacific Ocean. The East China Sea is in the northeast, while the Taiwan Strait and the South China Sea are in the southwest. Off the east coast, Taiwan faces the Pacific and, farther south, the Philippine Sea.

Opposite: **Chingshui Cliffs are among Taiwan's most dramatic stretch of coastline.**

Shadau beach is located in Kending National Park on Hengchun Peninsula.

Mountains and Earthquakes

Earth's outer layer is broken up into giant pieces called tectonic plates that fit together like a jigsaw puzzle. These plates are slowly moving. All the islands off the coast of Asia are located on a line where two tectonic plates come together. As these plates have rubbed together over millions of years, mountains have been pushed up. This movement of the plates also causes frequent earthquakes, including a devastating quake in Taiwan in 1999.

Taiwan is dominated by mountains, with the Central Mountain Range running down the center of the island like a spine from north to south. Many of the peaks tower more

The Central Mountain Range has more than one hundred peaks.

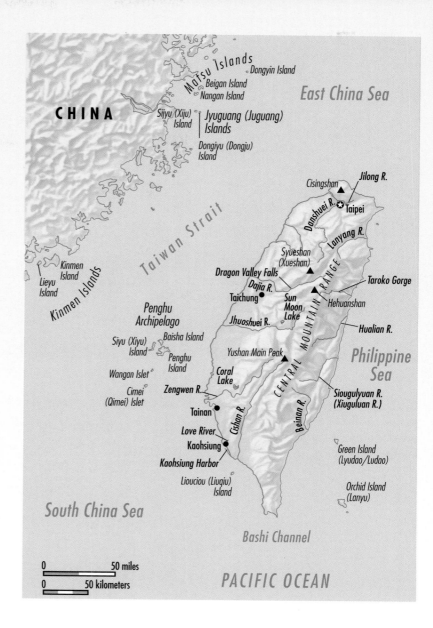

Taiwan's Geographic Features

Area: 14,015 square miles (36,300 sq km)

Greatest Length: 245 miles (394 km)

Greatest Width: 89.5 miles (144 km)

Bordering Countries: None

Coastline: 973 miles (1,566 km)

Highest Elevation: Yushan (Jade Mountain), 12,966 feet (3,952 m)

Lowest Elevation: Sea level

Average Annual Precipitation: 99 inches (252 cm)

Average July Temperature: 86°F (30°C)

Average January Temperature: 65°F (18°C)

than 10,000 feet (3,000 meters). At 12,966 feet (3,952 m), Yushan, or Jade Mountain, is the highest point in Taiwan and also the highest mountain in Southeast Asia. The forested slopes of the Central Mountain Range offer rugged scenic beauty. When Portuguese explorers first saw the island in the

Liyu Lake is located south-east of Hualien. It is a popular area for camping, boating, and hiking.

sixteenth century, they named it *Ilha Formosa*, meaning "beautiful island." It continued to be known as Formosa until the twentieth century.

Taiwan's Regions

Northern Taiwan has become a favorite getaway region for Taiwan's city dwellers. The area has intriguing rock formations, as well as hot springs that promise a soothing escape from a hectic workweek. Vacationers are also drawn to sun-drenched beaches. They enjoy boating in coastal waters and visiting offshore islands like Keelung and Turtle Island.

The eastern region of Taiwan is isolated from the rest of the island by the Central Mountain Range. This is the wildest landscape on Taiwan, with towering seaside cliffs facing the Pacific and deep valleys carved by swift rivers. The Taiwanese call this area Pure Land, a reference to the Buddhist image of paradise. It is the least developed region of Taiwan and the least crowded, with only about 10 percent of the population. Many of the people living in eastern Taiwan are members of the indigenous tribes who occupied the entire island before the Chinese arrived. In the southeast, the rugged land gives way to a flatter region of rice paddies.

Taroko Gorge

On an island known for its scenic beauty, the number-one tourist attraction is Taroko Gorge. Some four million years ago, the movement of the region's two tectonic plates pushed up huge blocks of marble. Over thousands of years, the Liwu River ate into the marble, carving this spectacular gorge. In some places, the marble cliffs tower so high above the gorge that they block out the sun. In other areas, the water has carved deep valleys. Elsewhere, the water tumbles over picturesque waterfalls. Nearly half the island's wild animal species can be found in Taroko Gorge, including black bears, wild boars, and Formosan rock macaques.

Two main crops of Taiwan are rice and betel nuts. The fertile Eastern Rift Valley provides the perfect growing conditions for these products.

The western region of Taiwan is not as wildly beautiful as the east, but it does boast some dramatic sites, including Yushan (Jade Mountain) and Sun Moon Lake, the island's largest body of water. The west is the most heavily populated region of Taiwan, the site of the island's largest cities. The west also has the island's best farmland. Bananas, pineapples, papayas, sugarcane, and rice all grow in the rich soil.

Looking at Taiwan's Cities

Kaohsiung (right) is Taiwan's second-largest city and its major seaport. In the last half of the twentieth century, the city was a symbol of Taiwan's rapid industrialization. Factories expelled billowy clouds of smoke and gases, polluting the air, the land, and the water. The Love River was little more than a chemical dump, and urban waste flowed past the beaches into Taiwan Strait.

Since the 1990s, Kaohsiung has been making a remarkable comeback. Industry is shifting toward high technology, and ambitious measures are under way to restore the city's beaches. Riverside parks, along with modern shops and restaurants, are replacing grim factories and rusting oil tanks. Many of the city's 1.5 million people believe, as the mayor states, that Kaohsiung will soon be the "Hawaii of Taiwan."

Taichung, Taiwan's third-largest city, has avoided the heavy industry and pollution of Kaohsiung, as well as the high-speed pressure of Taipei, the nation's capital. Many Taiwanese consider this the island's most livable city, with its clean air, mild climate, and slower pace. It is a city of picturesque streets and lanes, with countless historic temples and other buildings. Although more than one million people now live in Taichung, the city's relaxed pace and simple layout make it seem small and uncrowded.

Tainan (left), the oldest city in the country, boasts many historical landmarks. In the 1600s, it became the country's first capital. Tainan houses some of Taiwan's first streets, a fort built by the Dutch, and the earliest temples dedicated to Matsu, the goddess of the sea. The city maintains its history in an array of traditional temples, relics, and ceremonies. Tainan is the fourth-largest city of Taiwan and, as such, has its modern side. There are shopping malls, luxury hotels, and other new facilities. Its industries produce metals, textiles, and machinery, and its new science park brings it straight into the twenty-first century.

The Penghu Islands lie between Taiwan and China in the Taiwan Strait. The beautiful islands are a popular tourist destination.

The islands of Taiwan Strait form a separate, widely scattered region. The largest of the three groups of islands is the Penghu Archipelago. Also known as the Pescadores ("fishermen's islands" in Portuguese), the sixty-four islands are spread over 37 miles (60 km) from north to south and 13.6 miles (22 km) from east to west. In contrast to Taiwan's mountainous terrain, these islands are dry and flat, covered with grass and brush. Twenty of the islands are inhabited, with a combined population of about ninety thousand. Occupied at different times by the Dutch, the Chinese, the French, and the Chinese Nationalists, the islands contain numerous historical sites, including forts, shrines, and temples. The archipelago was recently named a national scenic area, and funds were invested to create beach resorts that would appeal to both Taiwanese and foreign visitors.

The Matsu Islands are a second important group in the Taiwan Strait. These islands are in the shadow of mainland China, located only a few miles from the mouth of China's Min River. After the Nationalists fled the mainland in 1949, they continued to use Matsu and Quemoy (now called Kinmen) as their first line of defense. The Chinese bombed the islands from time to time until 1958, when the U.S. Navy began patrolling the strait. Most of the nine thousand people who make their homes on the eighteen Matsu Islands live by fishing, and their picturesque villages have changed little in modern times.

Kinmen, located just 1 mile (1.6 km) off the mainland coast, has been called a garden built on top of a fort. In spite of its important position in the battle between the Nationalists and the mainland Chinese, the people of the Kinmen Archipelago have created tree-lined streets, pleasant lakes, and forest reserves. This archipelago is made up of fifteen islands with a total population of about forty-five thousand.

Unusual Souvenirs

The main island of Kinmen offers some of the most unusual souvenirs in all of Taiwan. The favorite item is a hard candy called *kung*, or "tribute," because it was once used to pay tribute when visiting the court of China. Peanut is the most popular of the many flavors of kung, which is sold from barrels on many street corners.

Other unusual souvenirs on Kinmen are a variety of metal toys and miniature weapons. They are made from melted-down artillery shells gathered from the Chinese bombardments. Since the shelling stopped more than thirty years ago, the price of these souvenirs has gone up steadily.

Waves from Typhoon Aere pound the shore in 2004 outside the city of Keelung. Typhoons can cause flash floods and landslides.

One Climate

Located between the Pacific Ocean and the South China Sea, Taiwan is famous for its sudden and dramatic changes in weather. The ocean brings abundant rainfall throughout the year, and there are two different monsoon seasons when heavy rain and wind batter the island. The northeast monsoon that swoops in from the Pacific brings heavy rainfall to the

"Great Wind"

The eastern side of Taiwan is buffeted by four or five typhoons every year between August and October. They are called *taifeng*, which means "great wind." This is a fitting name for storms that can produce winds of 150 miles (250 km) per hour and deliver up to 12 inches (33 cm) of rain in twenty-four hours.

In 2001, five typhoons hit Taiwan, claiming more than three hundred lives and producing $20 billion in damage. One of the worst storms of the past century was Typhoon Mindulle, which swept across central and southern Taiwan on July 1, 2004. Damage was particularly severe in Taichung and the surrounding countryside.

The Earthquake of 1999

The worst earthquake in modern Taiwanese history occurred on September 21, 1999. The magnitude 6.9 quake was centered in almost the exact middle of Taiwan. The strong quake did extensive damage, and many poorly constructed buildings were leveled. More than two thousand people died.

The world reacted with goodwill, and donations flooded in from other countries. Various religious organizations in Taiwan, particularly Buddhist, were on the scene immediately, and in some cases responded faster than the government. Today, the damaged areas have been rebuilt, and there is little evidence of the disaster.

northern and eastern regions between October and March. The southwest monsoon produces heavy rains on the western side of the island from May or June until August or September. These rains average just under 100 inches (250 centimeters) per year.

Summers are hot. Between May and September, the temperature averages 86 degrees Fahrenheit (30 degrees Celsius). The air is very humid, turning cities into steam baths. Summer is also the time of year for typhoons, storms with fierce wind and driving rain.

Winters are brief and mild, with temperatures usually above 60°F (16°C) near sea level, although the mountain peaks are often topped with snow. April, May, October, and November are the most pleasant months.

Preserving Nature's Gifts

WHEN MANY TAIWANESE BUSINESSES INSTITUTED A five-day workweek in 2001, people began using their weekends to get away from noisy, crowded cities. They flocked to the beaches and harbors on the west coast or crossed the island to the hiking trails and parks. This weekly exodus had two results. First, it renewed the Taiwanese people's fascination with the natural world. Second, it made it apparent to many people how rapidly the island's plants, wild animals, and scenic vistas were being lost to sprawling cities, industries, and paved roads.

Opposite: **The hawksbill turtle lives in the coral reefs that surround Taiwan.**

The Hsitou Forest Recreation Area offers a welcome change from Taiwan's bustling cities.

The Taiwanese now realize that their economic miracle has been a mixed blessing. In a remarkably short time, they have created one of the highest standards of living in the world. But the pollution and massive construction have taken a toll. The Taiwanese now feel they are in a race against time—a race to save nature's gifts from disaster.

Taiwan's Wildlife

The forested mountain slopes of Taiwan offer protection for the island's dwindling wildlife population. In spite of the shrinking habitat, the island still has seventy species of mammals, ninety kinds of reptiles, five hundred species of birds, and eighteen thousand types of insects. The lakes, streams, and coastal waters hold 2,700 kinds of fish.

Visitors to the Chitou Forest Recreation Area can see green bamboo, winding trails, giant trees, and more. The forest is home to fifty species of bamboo.

Formosan black bears usually live alone. They mark their territory with scratches on tree bark.

Many of Taiwan's mammals are unique to the island, having evolved in isolation from the mainland. The largest of the mammals is the Formosan black bear. The black bear lives at altitudes above 6,500 feet (2,000 m). It weighs up to 440 pounds (200 kilograms) and sports long, curved nails on its five-toed paws that enable it to dig out roots and insects. The Formosan black bear is almost impossible to spot, both because it is good at eluding people and because only a few remain on the island. The loss of habitat and illegal hunting have reduced the bear's numbers to about 250.

The number of Formosan rock macaques is growing. Some have lost their normal fear of humans and chase people who have food for them.

Another of the island's well-known mammals is the Formosan rock macaque. The macaque is a medium-sized primate with a reddish face and fur that changes color with the seasons. It measures about 40 inches (100 cm) in length, including the tail, and usually weighs less than 18 pounds (8 kg). Formosan macaques live on forested mountain slopes at altitudes below 10,000 feet (3,000 m). The largest populations are in national parks.

The Formosan pangolin, another of Taiwan's unique mammals, looks something like a cross between an armadillo and an anteater. This shy, slow-footed animal sleeps during the day and hunts for insect colonies at night. It uses its long, sticky tongue to snatch its insect meals. The pangolin responds to fright by rolling up in a ball and playing possum. If that doesn't work, the little 10-pound (45-kg) animal can lash out with its tail, which is covered with sharp-edged scales. And, like a skunk, it can also release a foul-smelling liquid to discourage attackers.

National Parks

Taiwan has six national parks. Here are some: Kending is a beach resort, where people can swim with tropical fish and dive among beautiful coral reefs. Migratory birds abound.

Yushan is home to the tallest mountain in Taiwan, as well as the Formosan salamander and the Formosan black bear. The park is dotted with mountain peaks, lakes, and waterfalls.

Yangmingshan (below) is a beautiful mountain park with a varied climate, where rare butterflies can be seen.

Taroko National Park is a spectacular gorge, known for being home to the Formosan rock macaque.

One of the favorite animals of mountain hikers is a little goat that is capable of leaping surprising distances. The Formosan serow stands only 3 or 4 feet (80 or 115 cm) high, but it can jump 7 feet (2 m). These unusual animals have crescent-shaped horns. They live deep in forests, where they dine on leaves and plants, licking rocks for salt. Serows mark their territory by releasing a liquid from glands near their eyes.

Many of Taiwan's mammals are rarely seen, even in national parks. Some are in serious danger of extinction. The Formosan cloud leopard, for example, has lost much of its habitat in the lower elevations of the Central Mountain Range, and people are afraid it may be extinct. There have been no verified sightings of the leopard since 1985, but hope persists that a few of the creatures remain secluded in the forests. Other hard-to-spot species include the Formosan wild bear and a type of deer called the Formosan sambar.

The Formosan serow stamps both forelegs when it is upset. Sometimes it also makes a screaming sound.

A man climbs a trail in a bamboo forest near Fenchihu. Some types of bamboo grow more than 160 feet (50 m) tall.

Year-Round Green

Even though Taiwan's wild areas have shrunk dramatically, nearly half the land area remains forested. It is estimated that Taiwan has more than four thousand species of plants, including about one thousand that exist only on the island.

Taiwan is green all year. The types of plants vary with altitude. In the lowlands, stands of bamboo are mixed with palm trees and tropical evergreen trees. Higher up the mountain slopes, between 2,000 and 6,000 feet (600 and 1,800 m), a variety of evergreens take over, including the camphor laurel, which was once common but has been harvested almost to extinction. Between 6,000 and 8,000 feet (1,800 and 2,400 m),

Chinese spinach is one of the many vegetables grown in Taiwan. It tastes similar to Western spinach.

the vegetation changes to cedars, cypress, junipers, rhododendrons, maples, and Japanese cedar. Above 7,500 feet (2,300 m), evergreen forests are dominant. In addition, ferns abound in large areas of the island. Taiwan has more than eight hundred types of fern, nearly twice the number found in all of North America.

Agriculture

Only about 25 percent of the land in Taiwan is suitable for farming. Nearly one hundred types of fruits and vegetables are grown in Taiwan, including bamboo shoots, cabbages, soybeans, tomatoes, watermelon, and cucumbers. Citrus fruits, bananas, mangoes, grapes, pineapples, peaches, and pears are also grown. Some farms specialize in flowers such as chrysanthemums, gladiolus, and prairie gentians. These flowers are sold in the cities.

The Delicate Plum Blossom

Taiwan's national flower is the plum blossom. This exquisite flower has soft pink or white blossoms that appear delicate but are actually quite hardy. The blossoms' ability to withstand rough weather was one reason the Taiwanese government chose the plum blossom as the national flower in 1964. Officials felt that the flower symbolized Taiwan's ability to cope with the unexpected. Some also pointed out that the flower's three groups of stamens—the parts that produce pollen—could stand for the Three Principles of the People, developed by Dr. Sun Yat-sen, the father of modern China. The three principles are nationalism, democracy, and social well-being.

Birdland

Taiwan's coastal marshes and sheltered coves make the island an attractive resting place for migrating birds. So far, five hundred bird species have been identified in Taiwan. Not surprisingly, bird watching has become a favorite hobby there, and bird-watching sites have been established throughout Taiwan.

Until recently, most Taiwanese felt that economic advancement was more important than protecting bird life. But a conservation movement began in the 1980s and has been slowly gathering momentum. The island now has fifty-three major bird habitats, covering nearly 20 percent of Taiwan. Nearly all of that area is protected from development.

Taiwan's birds include two very small owl species. The 6-inch (18-cm) Scops owl has yellow eyes and gray, black, and buff feathers. The collared owl is even smaller and is sometimes taken home as a pet. The Formosan blue magpie is a large bird, 25 inches (64 cm) long. It is bright blue and has large, white feathers in its tail. Taiwan is home to fourteen bird species found nowhere else in the world. The most famous is the Mikado pheasant, which is featured on the new Taiwan $1,000 bill.

Among the rare species that visit Taiwan, the black-faced spoonbill may have come closest to extinction. It is estimated

The Scops owl lives in mountain forests and woodlands. It is endangered because it has lost much of its habitat.

Strictly for the Birds

In 2001, the city of Taipei purchased 148 acres (60 hectares) of rice fields and allowed the land to return to its natural state. Within two years, this land, now known as Guandu Nature Park, had reverted to a wetland region of tall grasses, trees, and small ponds. The Wild Bird Society of Taipei manages the site, carefully monitoring visitors to protect the birds that live there.

People can look for great herons, gray herons, green-winged teals, and marsh harriers from three shelters at the park. They might also spot rare species, such as black-tailed godwits and ibises.

that only about three hundred black-faced spoonbills remain in the world. Two hundred have wintered near the Zengwen River. A favorite species among bird-watchers is the fairy pitta. Only about two thousand fairy pittas exist in the world, and many build their summer nests in Taiwan. The Taiwanese call it the "eight-colored bird" because of its multicolored feathers.

The clown wrasse lives in the coral reefs around Taiwan. Like many saltwater fish, the clown wrasse is quite colorful.

Underwater Life

Taiwan's coastal waters abound with tropical fish, while deeper waters near the island support a variety of game fish. Taiwan's rivers are home to more than 150 species of fish. Overfishing and pollution have taken their toll of Taiwan's marine life. An estimated twenty fish species are now on the endangered list.

Many of Taiwan's saltwater fish can be found among the coral that encircles the island. Coral reefs are colorful ecosystems that flourish in warm, shallow water. While coral are found in all of Taiwan's coastal waters, an area near Kending in the south is most famous. There, a coral reef stretches along the coast for 37 miles (60 km). It is home to more than half the species of coral found in the world. Giant brain corals grow near the shore, while deeper water is home to soft coral and grasses that flow back and forth with the current.

Coral reefs are fragile. They depend on a delicate balance of factors, including water temperature, sunlight, and nutrients. Some corals in Taiwan have suffered severe damage from the dirt, sewage, and garbage that have run off the land. The construction of a nuclear power plant also threatens corals by releasing heated water.

Some efforts to stop the damage, including the establishment of Kending National Park, have begun to help. The government has also banned the use of dynamite for fishing and has established stiff fines for harming the reef.

Sun Moon Lake

Sun Moon Lake, the largest body of freshwater in Taiwan, was hit hard by the 1999 earthquake. Hotels there were leveled, roads destroyed, and temples crushed. Yet out of this destruction came improved facilities at the lake. The new buildings were better than the old ones. New nature paths were created, docks restored, and scenic areas established.

Sun Moon Lake is now a favorite tourist spot. People come from all over to enjoy the spectacular landscape, high forested mountains, and fine year-round weather. Both motorboats and rowboats are popular. Some visitors go on hikes that take hours, while others simply enjoy short strolls along the lake.

Protecting the Environment

Many new parks have been created in Taiwan in recent years. This park in Taipei is a favorite for both visitors and residents.

The Taiwanese showed little interest in protecting the environment until the 1980s. Then citizens groups took the lead in demanding government action and in launching voluntary programs. The island now has nineteen nature reserves, which cover 159,329 acres (64,477 ha), and fourteen wildlife refuges,

The Butterfly Kingdom

Taiwan's warm, moist climate supports a large and remarkably varied butterfly population. More than four hundred butterfly species, including the Indian leaf butterfly above, have been identified—roughly fifty of these found only on Taiwan. They range in size from the tiny gossamer butterfly, which is less than an inch long, to the bird wing, a large, pearl-colored butterfly.

The Butterfly Valley near the town of Meinung welcomes as many as 50 million silver-veined yellow butterflies in the summer. They come to feast on the blossoms of chestnut trees. In Maolin, outside Kaohsiung, millions of striped blue crow butterflies create a purplish haze in the forests.

As with the other plants and animals in Taiwan, the number of butterflies has declined. In the past, people caught butterflies to use in art or crafts, or to sell to collectors in other countries. Roughly 10 million butterflies were exported every year.

The government has now protected several species by making it a crime to capture them. In spite of the losses, Taiwan is still considered the "butterfly kingdom."

which cover another 61,285 acres (24,801 ha). These refuges include a breeding ground for terns at the Cat Islets Seabird Refuge and the Wangan Island Green Turtle Reserve, both on the Penghu Islands. There are also twenty-four forest reserves, six national parks, and twenty-eight wildlife habitats.

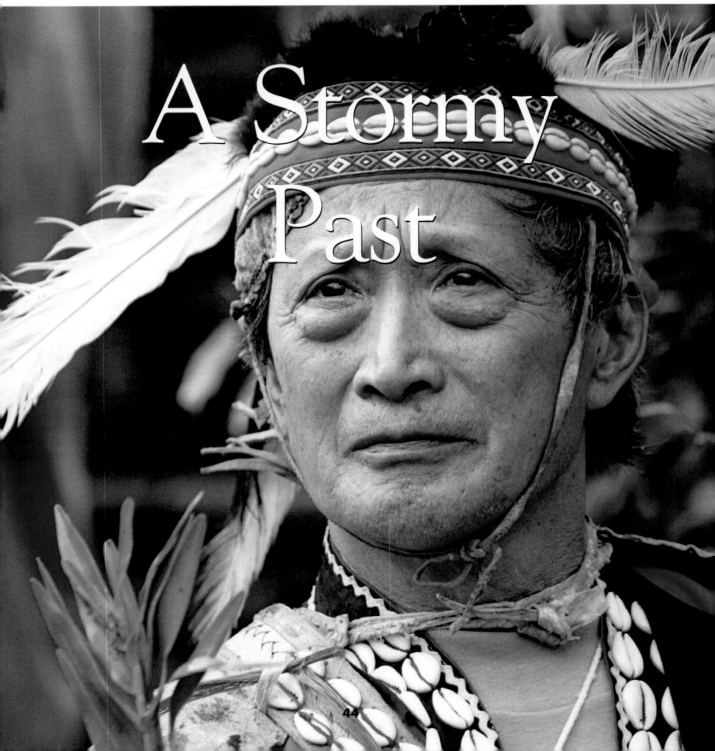

A Stormy Past

THROUGHOUT ITS HISTORY, SEVERAL DIFFERENT NATIONS and groups of people have found Taiwan appealing. People from mainland China have frequently seen the island as a place of escape or as a land of opportunity. Others have wanted Taiwan for its location—a crossroads between the Philippines and China and between the Philippines and Japan. The Chinese, Portuguese, Dutch, Spanish, and Japanese all have controlled it for a time, and pirates from both China and Japan used the island for a base.

No one seemed able to establish peace and order for long, largely because the people of Taiwan did not like being

Opposite: **An aboriginal Tsou elder offers a sacred plant to the God of War during a Mayasvi ceremony. This is the most important festival in the Tsou calendar.**

Many nations have tried to control Taiwan over the centuries. The Chingshui Cliffs north of Hualien is a challenging place for any outsider to land.

controlled by outsiders. Finally, in the past few years, the Taiwanese have achieved a large measure of the independence and democracy they had longed for. But the giant, mainland China, remains poised on their doorstep.

The Original People

Scientists have found more than five hundred prehistoric sites around Taiwan and on the three island groups offshore. Some of these sites date back ten thousand years. From artifacts such as shell mounds, red pottery, and decorated bronze tools, the scientists have concluded that the islands' earliest inhabitants were Malayan-Polynesian groups who came from the Pacific islands and Southeast Asia. Some sites also suggest a few early groups came from mainland China.

Four Paiwan boys from Tona pose for a photo. The Paiwan people are one of the indigenous groups that make up Taiwan's population. They are famous for their woodcarvings.

Today, the descendants of eleven indigenous, or native, groups make up about 2 percent of Taiwan's population. Modern Taiwanese refer to the native people as aborigines, or original people. Like the Native Americans of the United States and Canada, these original people are working hard to preserve their rich and varied cultural history.

This painting by Julian Oliver Davidson is titled *Chinese Pirates Attacking a Trader*. Pirates often hid in Taiwan's sheltered coves.

Who's in Charge?

In the fifteenth century, settlers from mainland China—mostly from Fujian Province—began arriving in Taiwan in fairly large numbers. They found the native people divided into two very different groups. One cluster of tribes lived on the fertile plains of southwest Taiwan, where they survived by hunting, fishing, and farming. The other group lived in the mountains. They moved about and were famous for their tattoos and for sometimes killing strangers.

Between the fourteenth and sixteenth centuries, both Chinese and Japanese pirates established bases in sheltered coves around the island. They would attack trading ships from China or Japan and then retreat to their island hideouts.

The first Europeans arrived in 1590, when the Portuguese established a trading post in northern Taiwan. They quickly gave it up, however. The Dutch were next to try. In 1622, they set up a trading post and fortress on the Penghu Islands.

When they were challenged by a powerful fleet from China's Ming dynasty, however, they agreed to move to southern Taiwan, at Anping, now part of Tainan.

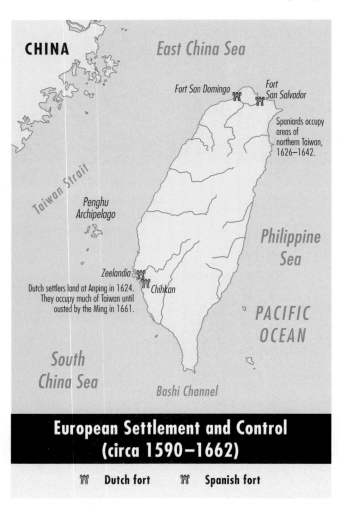

Dutch settlers land at Anping in 1624. They occupy much of Taiwan until ousted by the Ming in 1661.

Spaniards occupy areas of northern Taiwan, 1626–1642.

European Settlement and Control (circa 1590–1662)

🏰 Dutch fort   🏰 Spanish fort

The government of the Netherlands gave only the Dutch East India Company the right to trade in the island's products. The company herded local Chinese and some aborigines into farming villages that specialized in growing sugarcane and harvesting camphor—a compound used in medicines—from the camphor tree. The villages paid heavy taxes. Missionaries tried to convert the Taiwanese to Christianity, and they succeeded in converting large numbers of the aborigines.

In 1626, the Spanish tried to move into Taiwan. The Spanish fought off attacks from the Dutch and held on to a trading post at Keelung and a smaller one at Danshui. Then, in 1642, many Spanish troops were called to the Philippines, and the Dutch overran the posts.

Despite the difficulties with Spain, throughout the 1600s the Dutch East India Company controlled three hundred Chinese and aboriginal villages, which proved to be a great economic success. At the same time, on the mainland of China, Manchu warriors from the north were moving in on the ruling Ming dynasty. To escape the turmoil, hundreds of mainland Chinese fled to Taiwan. The Dutch welcomed them and provided them with tools, seeds, and oxen. The newcomers were grateful at first, but soon they began agitating for ownership of the land they farmed. The Dutch East India Company refused and even introduced a stiff new tax in 1652. Furious, the Chinese revolted. But the untrained, poorly armed peasants had no chance against the well-armed Dutch. An estimated six thousand Chinese were killed.

The Dutch built a fortress on the Penghu Islands. In the 1600s, the Dutch had forts and trading posts around the world.

Commodore Matthew Perry in an engraving by P. Haas. Perry thought Taiwan would serve as a good base for the United States in East Asia.

The Chinese Period

As the Manchus gained control from the tottering Ming dynasty, remnants of the Ming armies continued to resist. One of their leaders, Jheng (Zheng) Cheng-gong, known in the Western world as Koxinga, vowed to restore Ming rule. Between 1646 and 1658, he raised an army of one hundred thousand and equipped it with three hundred boats. After raiding coastal towns, he turned his attention to Taiwan. In 1661, after a long fight, he drove the Dutch out of Taiwan.

Koxinga's triumph was welcomed by the island Chinese, but it was short-lived. He became ill and died suddenly at the age of thirty-eight. His son and grandson remained in power for another twenty years, but their inept rule angered the people. Few of the island Chinese were sorry when the Manchu, or Qing, took control of Taiwan in 1684 and made it part of China's Fujian province. Although Koxinga did not rule Taiwan for long, he is still regarded as a popular hero for freeing the island from the Dutch.

The Qing ordered some one hundred thousand Chinese back to the mainland and tried to stop future immigration. The island was always restless and unruly, and the Qing were never able to gain stable control. During the 212 years of Qing rule, there were more than a hundred major uprisings and revolts. The unrest did not end the island's economic prosperity. Illegal immigrants continued to arrive from the mainland. Farms that had been controlled by the Dutch East India Company slowly fell into private hands. The fertile, moist land supported sugar plantations, rice fields, and tea plantations.

By the nineteenth century, Western nations, especially Britain, France, and the United States, noticed that Taiwan lay in a strategic position. The British stationed warships off the coast of Taiwan. Then, in the 1850s, U.S. naval commander Matthew Perry urged the American government to take control of it. But the island remained unruly, and it was hard for any nation to create stability and order.

One ongoing problem arose from the many shipwrecks along Taiwan's rocky shores. The sailors who survived the wrecks were often beaten or imprisoned by the Taiwanese. Sometimes they were even beheaded. The Europeans responded by bombarding coastal towns. However, the Qing dynasty government paid little attention to the trouble. It was having enough difficulty resisting the power of the European nations on the mainland. The declining power of the Qing, combined with the Taiwanese treatment of shipwrecked sailors, led to the takeover of the island by Japan.

Japanese Rule

In 1871, a Japanese ship sank on the southeast coast of Taiwan, and sixty-six men made their way to shore. An aboriginal tribe, the Botan, slaughtered fifty-four of them, and the Qing government did nothing. Japan responded in 1874 by sending twenty-five hundred soldiers to the island. After some military action against the Botan, the Qing government agreed to pay compensation to the sailors' families.

The incident shook up the Qing government, which acted to create some stability. In 1885, Taiwan was made China's twenty-second province. A new governor strengthened the island's defense system and tax structure. Telegraph lines were installed, a post office was opened, the first railroad line was started, and Western-style schools were established.

In 1894, Japan took advantage of China's obvious weakness to invade Korea, which then was controlled by China. The resulting Sino-Japanese War ended in a humiliating defeat for China. The Treaty of Shimonoseki in 1895 forced China to transfer Taiwan and the Penghu Archipelago to Japan.

The Taiwanese were shocked to hear that their island now belonged to Japan. A group of educated Taiwanese led the way

Tensions between the Chinese and the Japanese escalated into war in 1894. Most of the fighting took place in China and Korea.

in forming the Taiwan Democratic Republic. They issued a declaration of independence modeled on the American declaration, stating that Taiwan was an independent nation.

The Japanese had no intention of granting independence. Their army took control of northern Taiwan and fought stiff resistance as they moved south. The Taiwanese had only ancient weapons and bamboo spears in their fight against a modern army. It is estimated that more than ten thousand soldiers and civilians were killed in the first five months of Japanese rule. The Taiwan Democratic Republic was crushed, and Japan remained in control for fifty years. Another anti-Japanese uprising in 1915 called the Tapani Incident claimed the lives of more islanders.

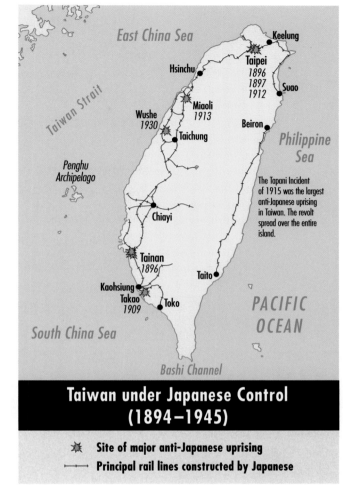

The Tapani Incident of 1915 was the largest anti-Japanese uprising in Taiwan. The revolt spread over the entire island.

Taiwan under Japanese Control (1894–1945)

✹ Site of major anti-Japanese uprising
⎯ Principal rail lines constructed by Japanese

Japanese rule was ruthless, but it did establish law and order. The Japanese were determined to modernize and "Japanize" the island. They built highways and railroads, schools, hospitals, and government buildings. But they also violently crushed any opposition and forced all islanders to learn Japanese, adopt Japanese names, and follow Japanese customs.

World War II led to dramatic changes in Taiwan. On October 25, 1945, a few weeks after Japan's surrender ended the war, Taiwan was returned to China. This return is celebrated as Retrocession Day.

In 1945, China was still embroiled in civil war. The Communist Party under the leadership of Mao Zedong was trying to wrest control from the Nationalist government, also known as the Kuomintang (KMT), headed by Chiang Kai-shek. When the Communists finally succeeded in ousting the Nationalists, the Nationalists fled to Taiwan. The Taiwanese at first cheered the arrival of the Nationalist Chinese. But they soon realized that after living under the brutal rule of the Japanese for so many years, they were now facing another dictatorship. A new governor, General Chen Yi, proved to be a disaster. His men looted Taiwanese homes and shops, and a 1947 event, known as the 2-28 Incident, turned into an anti-KMT riot that was ruthlessly crushed.

After the Communists won the civil war, they established the People's Republic of China (PRC) in October 1949. Chiang Kai-shek's Nationalist government, which was

The 2-28 Incident

On February 27, 1947, the police arrested a woman for selling cigarettes illegally and then beat the woman until she fell to the ground unconscious and bleeding. The event led to a riot that, the next day, turned into an anti-government rebellion. The KMT crushed the uprising, killing up to thirty thousand Taiwanese. To this day, the incident symbolizes popular feeling against KMT rule. In 1997, February 28 was declared a national holiday, and a new park in Taipei was renamed the 2-28 Peace Park.

Chiang Kai-shek visiting
Taipei in 1955

officially called the Republic of China (ROC), moved to
Taiwan. Chiang managed to keep control of Matsu, Kinmen,
and Wuchiu—islands a few miles off the coast of the mainland. These small islands remain Taiwan's first line of defense
against China.

Despite the cruelty of Chiang Kai-shek's government, the KMT's economic policies transformed the island from a prosperous agricultural society to an industrialized urban nation. By the mid-1970s, Taiwan had one of the highest living standards in Asia. Throughout Chiang Kai-shek's long rule, his KMT received vital support from the United States. During the Korean War, the United States promised it would help Taiwan if China invaded.

Gradually, U.S. policy changed as American leaders recognized mainland China's growing importance. In 1965, the United States stopped giving financial aid to Taiwan. In 1979, the United States withdrew its recognition of Taiwan

Holding the Giant at Bay

Twice during KMT rule, Taiwan barely avoided invasion by the Chinese. In October 1949, ten thousand Communist troops landed on Kinmen Island (known then as Quemoy), only about 3 miles (5 km) off the coast of the mainland. After a fierce battle that claimed fifteen thousand lives on both sides, the ROC air force and navy drove off the invaders.

In 1958, the Chinese again prepared to invade Kinmen (right), bombarding the island with an estimated five hundred thousand artillery shells. The United States sent jet aircraft, anti-aircraft missiles, and aircraft carriers to Taiwan. The "August 23rd Artillery War" ended without an invasion, but at a cost of three thousand civilian lives and one thousand ROC troops.

Taiwan and the United Nations

The long tug-of-war between Taiwan and mainland China is reflected in the debate over which one should be in the United Nations (UN). Almost every nation in the world belongs to the UN, which is dedicated to keeping peace across the globe. When the UN was formed in 1945, China was still ruled by Chiang Kai-shek and the Nationalists. At that time, China, Great Britain, the United States, France, and the Soviet Union were the major world powers, and those five countries were given permanent seats on the UN Security Council. But Chiang Kai-shek soon lost control of China to the Communists. He and the other Nationalists fled to Taiwan.

What happened to their place at the UN?

Through the 1950s and 1960s, Taiwan continued to hold China's seat, thanks to strong backing from the United States. But other countries, including mainland China, insisted that the UN face the reality that Taiwan was not China. In 1971, the United Nations expelled Taiwan and replaced it with mainland China. The UN decision strengthened Beijing's claim that it represents the real China and that Taiwan is merely a province.

and recognized instead the People's Republic of China. The U.S. government, however, did promise to support Taiwan if attacked by the mainland.

Chiang Kai-shek died in 1975 at the age of eighty-seven. (His widow, Madame Chiang Kai-shek, died in 2003 at age 105!) His son, Chiang Ching-kuo, was elected president in 1978 and remained president until his death in 1988. Chiang Ching-kuo's vice president, Lee Teng-hui—the first native-born Taiwanese to hold high office—took over as president.

Toward Democracy

After Chiang Kai-shek's death, Taiwan gradually moved toward democracy. While Lee Teng-hui was pushing for democratic reforms, Taiwan's relationship with mainland China remained a troubling issue. During Taiwan's first truly democratic presidential election in 1996, China launched a series

President Lee Teng-hui addresses government officials in front of a portrait of Sun Yat-sen, the father of modern China.

of "test" missiles within a few miles of the Taiwanese coast to discourage voters from reelecting Lee. When he was reelected and visited the United States, the Chinese threatened to launch a nuclear missile at Los Angeles.

In 1998, Beijing began to soften its approach toward Taiwan. But Lee angered China again in 1999 when he stated his belief that China and Taiwan are separate countries. This stance even alarmed some Taiwanese.

In 2000, Taiwan took another important step toward democracy when Chen Shui-bian, the leader of the new Democratic Progressive Party, was elected president, ending fifty-five years of KMT rule. His election infuriated the Chinese further, and they continue to insist on a "one country, two systems" solution. But Taiwan has been governing its own affairs for more than fifty years. The people of Taiwan remain distrustful of Beijing, and a solution still seems far off.

President Chen Shui-bian is the first president of Taiwan who is not a member of the KMT. Chen is committed to the idea that Taiwan and China are separate, independent nations.

Building a Democracy

T HE PEOPLE OF TAIWAN SUFFERED THROUGH FIFTY YEARS of the often-brutal government of Chiang Kai-shek's KMT. Still, the roots of the island's democracy are intertwined with the history of the KMT. That history goes back to the late nineteenth century.

Opposite: **The Taipei 101 is the world's tallest building. It is 1,671 feet (509 m) high.**

A Troubled History

In the 1890s, a young physician, Dr. Sun Yat-sen, was deeply disturbed by the cruelty of the Qing dynasty rulers and by the humiliating loss of Taiwan to Japan in 1895. Sun tried to launch a democratic revolution on the mainland. When it failed, he went into exile from 1895 to 1911, living in both Europe and North America. During this period, he announced his Three Principles of the People: nationalism (*minzu*), democracy (*minguan*), and social well-being (*minsheng*).

In 1911, a military uprising at Wuchang in China triggered the revolution that ended the tottering Qing dynasty and marked the end of five thousand years of rule by emperors in China. Sun rushed back to China and was named president of a provisional government under the

Chiang Kai-shek (left) and Sun Yat-sen pose for a photograph. They worked together to unify China.

Dr. Sun Yat-sen

In mainland China, Sun Yat-sen (right) is called the Father of the Revolution, and in Taiwan he is revered as the Father of China's modern nation. Because China was so splintered by rival warlords and political factions, he never saw his dream of a unified and democratic China come to pass. But his "Three Principles of the People" is a basic part of the political philosophy of Taiwan and also of the Communist government in mainland China.

Kuomintang. The next year, 1912, became Year One of the calendar still used in Taiwan, and it was the beginning of the Republic of China (ROC).

The creation of the ROC did not lead to unity. The southern provinces became independent as part of the republic, but in the north, large areas were controlled by powerful warlords. In 1917, Sun placed Chiang Kai-shek in charge of an academy to train KMT army officers. Both men tried to form alliances with the Communists and others and to wrest power from the warlords. When Sun died of cancer in 1925, Chiang Kai-shek replaced him and spent the next twenty years trying to unify China.

A Family's Long Reach

Although Sun Yat-sen was born in 1866, his family's influence continued into the start of the twenty-first century. His widow, Soong Ching-ling, who was about twenty years younger, became an official in China's Communist Party. Her sister, Soong Mei-ling (1898–2003), was better known as Madame Chiang Kai-shek. She influenced KMT and Taiwanese affairs almost until her death in New York City at the age of 105.

After World War II and the Communist takeover of mainland China, Chiang Kai-shek moved his KMT party and government to Taiwan. It was a harsh dictatorship until after Chiang's death in 1975. His son, Chiang Ching-kuo, softened KMT rule. In 1986, the KMT decided to allow another political party—the Democratic Progressive Party (DPP)—to form. This amounted to a political revolution. After decades of being the only political party, the KMT was making room for opposition. The following year, Chiang Ching-kuo announced the end of martial law—using the military to keep order—which had been in effect for forty years.

In the next few years, the DPP grew steadily, winning seats in the legislature and the local government. Then, in 1996, two other parties emerged. The New Party candidate won 15 percent of the vote for president. Taiwan took another major step toward democracy when DPP candidate Chen Shuibian was elected president in 2000, ending fifty-four years of KMT rule.

Chiang Kai-shek poses with his wife, Soong Mei-ling, in 1964. Madame Chiang Kai-shek played an important role in Taiwanese politics.

The Structure of the Government

Taiwan's government structure is based on the KMT constitution, which was approved in 1947. The chief of state is the

The Kaohsiung Incident

The KMT's gradual surrender to democracy often received a shove from the people. In 1979, for example, a group of Taiwanese, inspired by the statements on human rights by U.S. president Jimmy Carter, organized a rally to celebrate International Human Rights Day. Two organizers were arrested and beaten by police for handing out leaflets promoting the event. The confrontation turned into a riot. Eight organizers, including Annette Lu, who is now vice president, were put on trial.

The incident highlighted the KMT's brutality. One of the accused, Lin Yi-hsiung, was tortured by the police. Early the following year, his twin daughters and mother-in-law were murdered. The murders were never solved.

The eight defendants were sentenced to long prison terms. But the government's actions during and after the Kaohsiung Incident increased the Taiwanese people's demands for greater democracy, and the KMT was slowly forced to yield.

president, who represents Taiwan in all foreign relations and state functions. In the past, he or she was elected to a six-year term by the National Assembly made up of KMT officials. The National Assembly has now been disbanded, and since 1996 the president has been elected by the people. Chen Shui-bian was elected president in 2000 and reelected in 2004. He chose the current vice president, Annette Lu, who had been imprisoned following the Kaohsiung Incident.

The president also appoints the premier, who administers government affairs and appoints the heads of Taiwan's ministries, or departments, including Defense, Economic Affairs, Foreign Affairs, Justice, and Transportation and Communication.

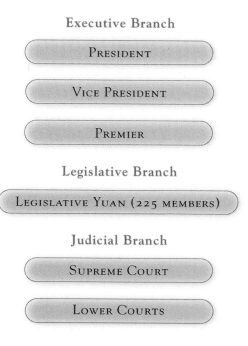

GOVERNMENT OF TAIWAN

Executive Branch

PRESIDENT

VICE PRESIDENT

PREMIER

Legislative Branch

LEGISLATIVE YUAN (225 MEMBERS)

Judicial Branch

SUPREME COURT

LOWER COURTS

The government is divided into five branches, or *yuan*. The Executive Yuan functions as a cabinet, headed by the premier, and is responsible for implementing government policy.

The Legislative Yuan, with 225 members, votes on new laws and programs. This branch also manages the budget and has the power to impeach the president or vice president.

The fifteen members of the Judicial Yuan oversee the court system and are responsible for civil, criminal, and administrative cases. In addition to the Supreme Court and lower courts, there is a Committee on the Discipline of Public Functionaries.

Taiwan's Anthem

The Taiwanese anthem is "San Min Chu I" ("The Rights of the People"). The lyrics come from a speech given by Dr. Sun Yat-sen in 1924. The music is by Cheng Mao-yun.

> "San min chu I," our aim shall be,
> To found a free land, world peace be our stand.
> Lead on comrades, vanguards ye are,
> Hold fast your aim, by sun and star,
> Be earnest and brave, your country to save,
> One heart, one soul, one mind, one goal!

The tests for Taiwan's civil servants and other government personnel are supervised by a twenty-one-member Examination Yuan, which also hires and manages government workers.

The watchdog branch is the Control Yuan. Appointed by the president, its task is to search out and remove any dishonest government workers or officials.

While the Taiwanese have overcome great obstacles to establish their democracy, the future remains uncertain because

Taiwan's premier, Yu Shyi-kun (first row center) poses with other members of the cabinet in 2005.

Taipei, the capital of Taiwan, is a thriving modern city.

of the unsettled relationship between the island and the mainland. China has toned down the threats and posturing, and trade between China and Taiwan is growing. The Taiwanese, with their higher standard of living and more educated people, appear to have little interest in seeing the island become a province of the mainland. It may be that the increasing economic ties will lead to the kind of compromise that political leaders have not been able to achieve.

Taiwan's Flag

The flag of Taiwan is, technically, the flag of the Republic of China. It was designed in 1928, when Chiang Kai-shek's Nationalists were in control of much of mainland China. The flag is red, with a white sun on a blue background in the upper left corner. The red stands for liberty and sacrifice. White symbolizes brotherhood and honesty. Blue represents purity, freedom, and government of the people.

Taipei: Did You Know This?

Taipei, the capital of Taiwan, is one of the busiest, fastest-moving cities in the world. It is also Taiwan's social, economic, and cultural capital. This sprawling city of three million is surrounded by a ring of mountains.

Taipei is only one hundred years old. As recently as 1960, it was a small agricultural town. The run-away economic growth that began in the 1970s was achieved at the cost of overcrowding, uncontrolled construction, and fierce pollution problems. The people have rebuilt their city since the 1990s. Traffic has been eased by the mass rapid transit system (MRT), considered the best subway system in Asia. Bus lanes on wide avenues and better taxi service have persuaded many drivers to leave their cars at home.

On the streets, everyone seems to be dressed in the latest fashions. People are friendly and helpful, even though the pace of life is so frenetic. European, American, and Japanese shops and boutiques offer brand-name goods. And few cities anywhere in the world can offer a greater number of outstanding restaurants.

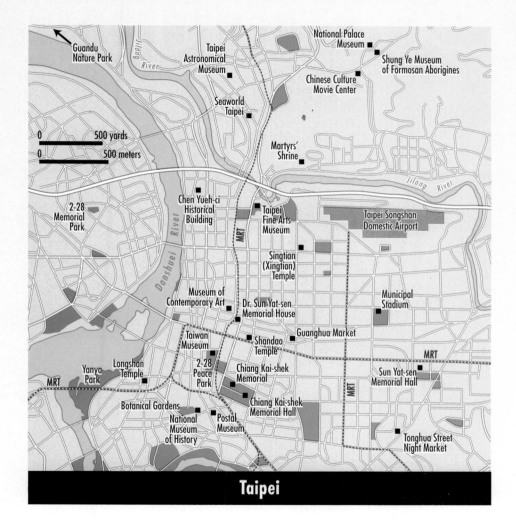

Taipei

Continuing the Economic Miracle

I N THE 1960S AND 1970S, THE LABEL "MADE IN TAIWAN" was familiar to people throughout the world. The phrase was found on low-cost products, such as T-shirts, shoes, textiles, toys, and sports equipment. In about twenty years, Taiwan had been transformed from an agricultural economy to an industrial one. In the 1980s, the island began its second economic miracle. This time it became a producer of high-tech electronics products, mostly for export.

Opposite: **Bicycles are one of the many products manufactured in Taiwan.**

Government and the Economy

Throughout the twentieth century, the government played a key role in creating Taiwan's remarkably successful economy.

Many Taiwanese work in the computer industry. This woman inspects a circuit board at a company in Taipei.

When Japan controlled Taiwan in the early twentieth century, the Japanese government constructed irrigation systems and introduced the heavy use of chemical fertilizers to make farms more productive. The government also oversaw the building of highways, railroads, harbors, and agricultural schools.

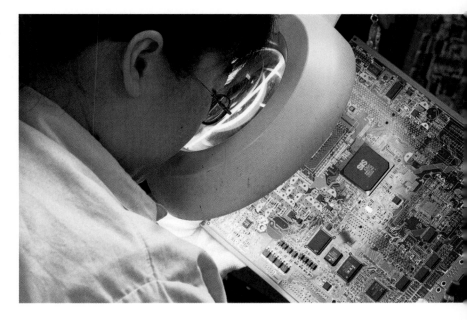

When the Nationalists took over Taiwan after World War II, they inherited a strong agricultural economy.

Chiang Kai-shek's Nationalist government concentrated on the development of heavy industry in Taiwan. The United States and Canada provided investments and technological help. The Taiwanese provided a hardworking labor force. The result was Taiwan's economic miracle. The country began exporting huge amounts of low-cost consumer goods, along with some food items. This made Taiwan increasingly wealthy, giving it one of the highest standards of living in the world.

In the 1970s and 1980s, Taiwan produced many low-cost goods such as televisions.

Taiwan's Silicon Valley

The Taiwan government established the Hsinchu Science-Based Industrial Park in 1980 in the city of Hsinchu, southwest of Taipei. The park has been a huge success from the beginning, and most of the island's output of electronics comes from there. Roughly 350 companies are located at Hsinchu, and many more are on a waiting list to get in. An estimated $25 billion in U.S. dollars has been invested, producing a yearly revenue of $20 billion. More than four-fifths of this money comes from companies producing computer components and other electronic goods.

Other countries in Asia have tried to establish similar parks but without the same success. In 1996, Taiwan opened a second park near Tainan, and a third is planned for Taichung in central Taiwan.

By 1980, Taiwan's business and government leaders saw that the country could not continue to rely on heavy industry. Environmental pollution was reaching disaster proportions. And many companies wanted to shift their operations to mainland China, the Philippines, or Southeast Asia, where lower labor costs would boost profits.

Once again, the government led the way in shifting Taiwan's economy. One major step was the creation of the Hsinchu Science-Based Industrial Park for companies making computer components and other electronic products. Through the 1980s and 1990s, the government gave tax breaks to companies that invested in the park. The government also provided funds and facilities for research and development, training, and technical support.

People and Languages

Aborigine women dressed in traditional clothing. Aborigines make up less than 2 percent of Taiwan's population.

for the daluren privileges and power. The sense of distrust between the two groups lingers, but it is expected to ease as more benshengren move into positions of political power.

The indigenous people, also known as aborigines, are called *yuanjhumin*. These descendants of the island's original people make up less than 2 percent of the total population. The government recognizes eleven aboriginal groups, with a total population of about 370,000. The Ami, the largest group,

Ethnic Divisions of Taiwan

Taiwanese	85%
Mainland Chinese	13.2%
Aborigine	1.8%

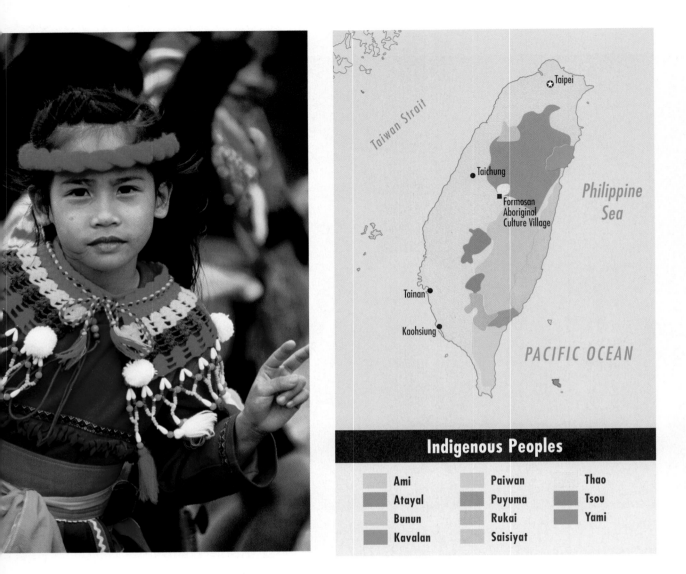

Indigenous Peoples

Ami	Paiwan	Thao
Atayal	Puyuma	Tsou
Bunun	Rukai	Yami
Kavalan	Saisiyat	

An aboriginal girl dressed in brightly colored clothing. Many Taiwanese aborigines proudly celebrate their heritage.

number about 150,000. They live in the mountains and valleys of Hualin County on the east coast. Smaller groups, like the Yami on Orchard Island and the Thao, who live around Sun Moon Lake, number only a few thousand. Other native groups include the Atayal, Bunun, Paiwan, Rukai, Saisiyat, Kavalan, and Tsou.

From the 1950s to the 1990s, little attention was paid to these groups. In the 1980s, people throughout the world took a new interest in their indigenous populations, including the aborigines of Australia and the Native Americans of North and South America, as well as the aborigines of Taiwan.

The aboriginal groups began making appeals to the Taiwanese government in the late 1980s, asking for help in addressing problems like unemployment and alcoholism. The government responded in 1992 with a six-year plan to promote aboriginal culture and to provide medical care, business loans, and legal advice. The government also made certain mountain areas into aboriginal reservations, banning the sale of the land to nonnatives.

These dancers are performing at the Taiwan Aboriginal Culture Park. Taiwan's earliest inhabitants were from the South Pacific.

The Aboriginal Culture Village

One project that has increased interest in the aboriginal way of life is the Formosan Aboriginal Culture Village, which is located in western Taiwan. The village is an unusual combination of amusement park and culture-study center, but it's a combination that seems to work. Houses and other village structures of each aboriginal group have been reconstructed, and there are demonstrations of crafts, food, dance, and religious celebrations. Visitors can also enjoy a variety of amusement park rides from merry-go-rounds to roller coasters, as well as restaurants serving Asian, Western, and aboriginal foods.

Traditional butterfly designs are being sewn by members of the Rukai tribe. Their crafts have become popular with tourists.

The government program launched a new era of appreciation for indigenous culture and crafts. Roads were built to connect isolated areas of the island, including native reservations, with urban centers. This has brought growing numbers of tourists to aboriginal villages. In the cities, native foods, music, and dance have become popular. Aboriginal designs now appear regularly in clothing and decorations.

Problems persist for Taiwan's aborigines, however. Their education and income levels lag behind those of the rest of the population. Unemployment and alcoholism continue to be problems, and the use of aboriginal languages is declining. In spite of these difficulties, the native people have taken renewed pride in their crafts and arts, which are also enjoying the appreciation of the Taiwanese and of foreign visitors.

Many signs in Taiwan are written in both Chinese and the Western alphabet.

The Languages of Taiwan

Visitors to Taiwan are often confused by the use of different English translations of Chinese names and words. A street in Taipei, for example, is called Zhongxiao, but the Chinese can also be transliterated to "Chunghsiao" or "Chung Hsiao." Another street name is spelled "Ta an," "Da an," or "Daan."

The reason for the confusion is that there are three different systems for the translation, or Romanization, of Chinese into English, and government authorities have not been able to agree on one. The Wade-Giles Romanization system is the oldest system. It was widely used until two easier systems were introduced. This book, like most American and European books about Taiwan, uses the Romanization system called Tongyong Pinyin, which was created in the 1990s. A similar system, called Hanyu Pinyin, has become the international standard for Mandarin, which is mainland China's official language. To keep matters as confused as ever, the Taipei government has made Tongyong Pinyin official for two languages spoken in Taiwan—Mandarin and Hakka—but not for a third, Taiwanese.

By now, you may be as puzzled as most American visitors to Taiwan are. And there is more confusion to come. For the purpose of this book, keep in mind that we are using Tongyong Pinyin throughout, with Hanyu Pinyin in parentheses when the spelling is different.

Competing Languages

Another thorny matter to sort out is the relationship between the Taiwanese and Chinese languages. When the Nationalists took control of Taiwan, Chiang Kai-shek's government heavily promoted Mandarin, even though few people on the island could speak it. Most islanders at the time spoke Hokkien, which was usually referred to as Taiwanese. Most islanders also spoke Japanese, which the government of Japan had tried to make the only language used on Taiwan.

In addition to Hokkien and Japanese, a minority of Taiwanese spoke Hakka, another Chinese language that is still used by about 10 percent of the population. Each of the aboriginal groups has its own language, all of which are very different from Chinese or Taiwanese.

During the forty years of tight Nationalist control, little was written in Taiwanese because of the government's efforts to suppress it. But Taiwanese endures, and about half the people prefer to use it, especially in the south and in rural areas.

Many older people in Taiwan speak Japanese because Japan controlled the island between 1895 and 1945.

Today, just about all Taiwanese under the age of sixty speak and write Mandarin (which is also the official language of China). Many older people still know Japanese, but its use has dropped steadily. Taiwanese students are required to learn English but, like most American students learning a foreign language, they tend to read and write it far better than they speak it. There is also some effort to revive Hakka, and there is a new TV station in that language.

Tonal Languages

The major languages used in Taiwan—Mandarin, Taiwanese, and Hakka—are all tonal languages. The speaker, by changing the pitch, or tone, of his or her voice within a syllable, changes the meaning of a word. Mandarin has four tones. Here is an example:

word	tone	meaning
ma	high tone	"mother"
ma	rising tone	either "numb" or "hemp"
ma	falling-rising tone	"horse"
ma	falling tone	"scold" or "swear"

How Do You Say . . . ?

Here are a few words and phrases in Mandarin:

Hello	*Ni hao*
(more polite)	*Nin hao*
Goodbye	*Zaijian*
Please	*Qing*
Thank you	*Xiexie*
Many thanks	*Duoxie*
What is your name?	*Nin guixing?*
My surname is . . .	*Wo xing . . .*
Does anyone here speak English?	*Zheli you ren hui shuo yingyu ma?*

Chinese Characters

Chinese languages and dialects do not use an alphabet. Instead, each word has its own character. Some dictionaries list more than 50,000 characters, but the most widely used dictionaries list only about 2,400. Add to this the fact that about one word in five has more than one pronunciation, and you know why a Chinese proverb says that it takes a lifetime plus a few years to learn the language.

An elderly person reads a prayer book written in Chinese. Each Chinese character is its own word.

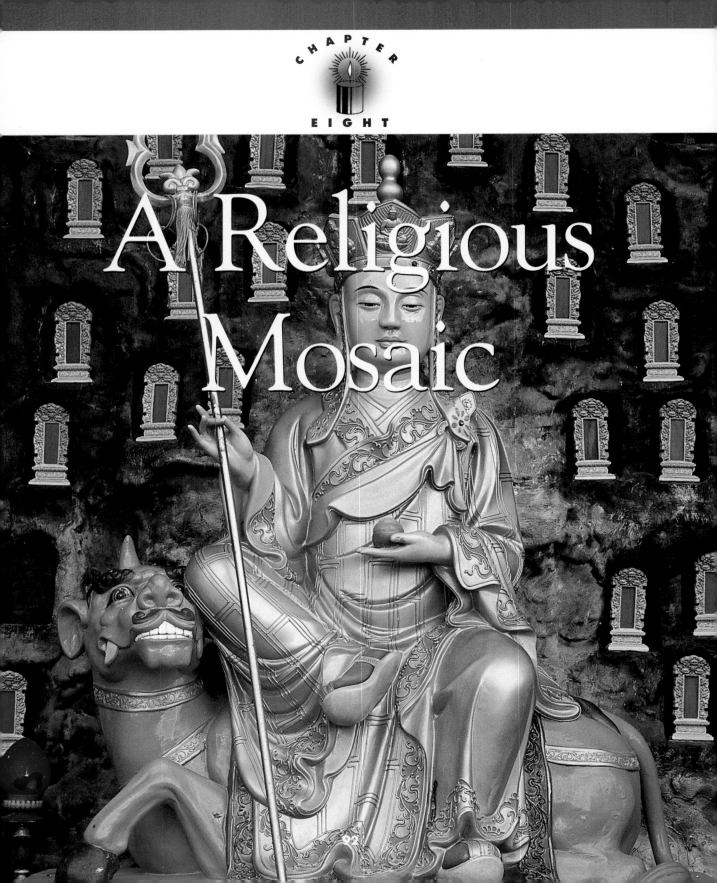

A Religious Mosaic

R ELIGION IN TAIWAN DOES NOT FIT INTO NEAT CAT-
egories. No one religion dominates. The three major belief
systems—Taoism, Buddhism, and Confucianism—have borrowed freely from each other and from folk religion. The
result is a mosaic: a mixture of many different pieces.

In Taiwan, religious practices are built into every person's
daily life in a variety of ways. A high school student on the way
to a tough exam will pause at the family's shrine to burn incense
to a favored ancestor. A banker prepares for a meeting by read-
ing the *Lunyu* (*Analects*) of Confucius. And a rice farmer on his
way home stops to leave a food offering at a village temple.

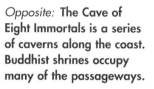

Opposite: **The Cave of Eight Immortals is a series of caverns along the coast. Buddhist shrines occupy many of the passageways.**

People make offerings at the Lung Shan Buddhist Temple.

Taiwan's Religions

Mixture of Buddhist, Confucian, and Taoist	93.0%
Christian	4.5%
Other	2.5%

While there is solemnity in the island's temples and rituals, there is also color, joy, and lots of noise. Not a week goes by without a festival, usually honoring a god's birthday. Hundreds of people join the parade that features some god's icon held high on a sedan—a portable chair designed to be hoisted in the air with poles—along with banging drums, pounding cymbals, and endless, deafening firecrackers.

The roots of Taiwan's major belief systems go deep into the history of mainland China. These belief systems became part of Taiwan's history in more modern times.

Eight young men carry the goddess Matsu. At her temple, they light firecrackers to celebrate.

Folk Religion

Just about every village and town practices folk customs connected to a person or event in that area. Temples are dedicated to any of the countless gods and goddesses that are part of Chinese folk culture. Some of these gods were real people. One of the most famous was the warrior Guan Yu, who has scores of temples dedicated to him all over Taiwan. Other popular deities are the God of Heaven, who represents justice; the God of the Earth, who oversees the harvest; and the House God, who guards new homes. By far the most popular of all the folk deities is Matsu.

The Folk Goddess Matsu

Matsu is the most popular folk deity in Taiwan. More than five hundred temples on the island are dedicated to her. Matsu is regarded as the goddess of the sea and she is the unofficial patron saint of the island.

Matsu's origins are uncertain, although most people agree that she was a real person named Lin Mo, who lived on an island off the coast of the mainland around A.D. 1000. Stories are told of her love of the sea and how she could be seen standing on the shore, dressed in red, guiding sailors through storms. She met her death at an early age, drowned during a storm. Some say she was seen flying to heaven dressed in red.

Soon after her death, people began praying to her for safety at sea. They also began building temples to honor her, first in China and then in Taiwan, Singapore, and Japan. Her birthday is on the twenty-third day of the third lunar month. The Matsu Festival, a long journey from her temple in Tachia to the Hsinkang Taoist temple, brings out thousands of pilgrims, accompanied by gongs, drums, and acrobats.

This Taoist design uses dragon imagery. It is at the Wenwu Temple at Sun Moon Lake.

Taoism

Taoism has more followers than any other religion in Taiwan. There are more than 4.5 million Taoists who worship at seven thousand temples around the island. Taoism, which is often mixed with folk beliefs and gods, is generally based on the *Tao Te Ching*, a work attributed to Lao-tzu, a somewhat mythical figure who lived in the sixth century B.C. The religion places an emphasis on individual freedom and harmony with nature. The central concept is called the *Tao*, being in harmony with all things in the universe without trying to impose one's will. This is also called *wuwei*, the idea of nonaction.

Over time, Taoism developed a religious branch separate from its more philosophical side. Religious Taoism borrowed heavily from Buddhism and folk religions. It became increasingly concerned with the afterlife and with achieving immortality.

Feng Shui

The practice of feng shui has been around for more than two thousand years, and it continues in Taiwan today. Feng shui is a way of placing objects in one's home or office to maximize positive energy and establish harmony and balance. In feng shui, some arrangements follow logical rules. For example, a stove and a refrigerator should not be placed together in such a way that hot and cold will collide. Other placement of objects is more mystical and doesn't make logical sense. People sometimes hire a feng shui master because they believe the master can help them achieve a contented home or a successful business.

When the Japanese ruled Taiwan, Taoists faced persecution, and many temples were transformed into Buddhist temples. Since 1949, Taoism has grown steadily. Many people notice that the temples project a carnival-like atmosphere. They are adorned with many exotic statues and a rainbow of bright colors. On the birthday of a deity, the temples explode with fireworks, gongs, drums, and bells.

Buddhist monks conduct a ceremony in Tinhau Temple in Tainan. Buddhism first came to Taiwan in the 1600s.

Buddhism

Buddhism began in India around 400 B.C., with a man named Siddhartha Guatama. By the time it reached China in the first century A.D., it had already split into two traditions. Those in the Hinyana division believe that Siddhartha was the one and only Buddha. They believe he was not a god but a man who had achieved perfection, which enabled him to escape the cycle of poverty.

In the Mahayana tradition, Siddhartha is seen as the reincarnation of an endless series of Buddhas, from the past through the present and far into the future. In Mahayan Buddhism, Buddhas became gods. They were beings who had transcended suffering and could hear the prayers of their followers. It was Mahayana Buddhism that came to China and eventually to Taiwan in around 1600.

Chung Tai Chan Temple

The massive Chung Tai Chan temple, near the town of Puli in western Taiwan, is one of the most remarkable structures on the island. After more than ten years of work, the temple was opened in 2001 as an international center for Buddhist research, culture, and arts. The building has won awards for its bold mixture of the traditional and the modern. One master craftsman spent years collecting jade for carvings on the building. Marble from fifteen countries was imported and pure teak used to build the seven-story pagoda in the middle of the temple. Modern touches include technology that allows visitors to pick out and light any one of the thousands of donor plaques that line the walls. Temple tours enable visitors to study historical, cultural, or religious aspects of Buddhism. The nuns and monks learn English from Westerners living in the temple so that they can guide tours in at least two languages.

Buddhism enabled people to think about ways of escaping suffering through reincarnation, or the rebirth of the soul in another body. Each time a soul is reincarnated, it comes closer to perfection. Many Chinese people were attracted not only to the beliefs of Buddhism, but also to the colored robes, the chanting, and the incense burning.

Confucianism

Confucianism is more a way of living than a religion, although there are hundreds of Confucian temples spread across Taiwan. The beliefs and values of Confucianism began with a Chinese scholar and teacher named Confucius (551–479 B.C.).

Over many centuries, Confucian thought and beliefs came to form the very foundation of Chinese culture and society. Confucius taught that society was made up of five kinds of relationships: ruler and subject, husband and wife, father and son, elder and younger family members, and friend and friend. Confucius believed that in each of these relationships, one person owes obedience to the other. Thus, the ruler expects to be obeyed by the subject, and the parent expects obedience from the son or daughter. Confucian thought also made the family the most important social unit, followed by friends and country.

Mencius (372–289 B.C.) was an early interpreter of Confucius. Mencius argued that people are born good and moral.

Confucius

Confucius was one of the most influential people in all of human history. He was born in 551 B.C. and lived during a period of war and upheaval in China. He came to believe that family, loyalty, and respect were central to society. In an attempt to restore harmony to Chinese life and bring about change, he taught his beliefs to others. It is estimated that he had explained his philosophy to more than three thousand students by the time of his death in 479 B.C., and that nearly two hundred of them became his disciples. They continued his teachings and preserved them in books.

The five classics of Confucianism are the *I Ching (Book of Changes)*, *Shijing (Book of Poetry)*, *Shujing (Book of History)*, *Liji (Book of Rites)*, and *Chuzu (Spring and Autumn Annals)*. The disciples published other collections of his work, but by far the most influential was the *Lunyu (Analects)*, a collection of his essays and dialogues with his students.

Confucianism became deeply engrained in the structure of society in China and, later, of society in Taiwan. It continues to shape individual character, family life, and social structure in Taiwan today. The individual, held in a tight web of relationships and obligations, feels secure. And from the ruler's point of view, the individual is obedient.

In Taiwan today, many people feel that their society has become too stiff and formal. Even in school, young people find themselves trapped in a system that depends largely on test scores. Western ideas of personal freedom and self-expression sometimes collide with traditional ideas of order and obedience. In spite of some conflict between the modern and the traditional, the close ties of family and friends continue to characterize Taiwanese life.

Taiwan's Temples

Taiwan's architecture is outstanding for its number and variety of temples. All temples, including folk religion temples, have certain architectural features in common. These include a rectangular shape, a front courtyard, and details like a curb in the doorway that keeps ghosts and evil spirits from entering.

The more than seven thousand Taoist temples are probably the most striking because of their bright colors, curved roofs, and parade of dragons, monkeys, and other animals along the ridges. Inside, Taoist temples are noisy beehives of activity, with devotees building fires of paper "ghost" money, burning incense, lighting firecrackers, or throwing crescent-shaped blocks to receive a yes-or-no answer about the future. Buddhist temples are less colorful than Taoist temples. They place greater emphasis on quiet prayer and reflection. Confucian temples lack the elaborate decorations of the Buddhist or Taoist buildings.

This Catholic church is located in the village of Tienhsiang near the Taroko Gorge. Spanish missionaries brought Catholicism to Taiwan.

Christianity in Taiwan

Nearly one million Taiwanese are Christian. They worship in about three hundred churches. Spanish missionaries brought Catholicism to the island in the late sixteenth century, and Dutch missionaries introduced Protestantism a few years later. After World War II, Mormons and Jehovah's Witnesses began to gain converts. In recent years, evangelical Christians have become more common. Today, about 25 percent of the Christians in Taiwan are Catholics. The rest are divided among the Protestant denominations.

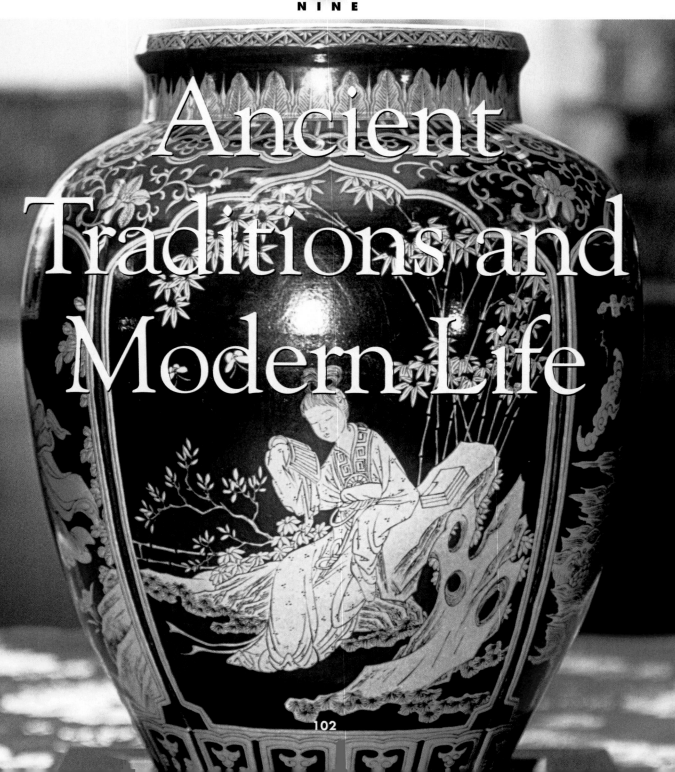

Ancient Traditions and Modern Life

TAIWANESE ART AND LITERATURE ARE BASED ON THE traditions of mainland China—traditions that often date back hundreds or thousands of years. But some artistic forms are unique to Taiwan, including the island's pop music, films, and modern dance. Besides the legacy of China, the work of Taiwanese artists and writers has been influenced by the island's bumpy ride through modern history: the fifty-year occupation by the Japanese, four decades of Chiang Kai-shek's Nationalist dictatorship, and the more recent struggle to build a democracy.

When you consider all these elements, it's no wonder that the central theme of many artists is a search for identity. Many film directors, novelists, poets, songwriters, and artists are engaged in a quest to discover what it means to be Taiwanese in the early years of the twenty-first century.

Opposite: **This Qing Dynasty vase dates back to the 1600s.**

Children in native dress at the Formosan Aboriginal Cultural Village. Taiwan has ancient traditions, but it is also a fast-paced modern country.

Painting

This painting, titled *Late Return from a Spring Outing*, is from the Ming Dynasty, 1494–1552. Like many Chinese paintings, it shows peaceful scenes of nature.

The National Palace Museum in Taipei has a timeline showing the history of art in China and in the world. The visitor goes through more than three-quarters of the timeline before reaching the great art of Europe—the rest is all China. That timeline is a startling illustration of China's long artistic history.

Long ago, Chinese painting began emphasizing brush technique rather than color as in Western art. Over many centuries, Chinese landscape paintings became more romantic and moody, with mist-covered mountains and serene waterfalls. Classical Chinese painting often shows scenes of nature, filled with peace and harmony.

This traditional art was transferred to Taiwan between the sixteenth and nineteenth centuries. After 1895, the Japanese introduced Western art to the island. In fact, an artist of Japanese ancestry, Ishikawa Kinichiro, became known as the father of modern Taiwanese art. Then, in the years after the Nationalists gained control of Taiwan, the island's

The National Palace Museum

The largest collection of Chinese art in the world is not in Beijing but in Taipei, in the National Palace Museum. The Chinese are not happy about it. Mainland Chinese who want to study the country's art history have to get special permission to travel to Taiwan. Here's how this happened:

As far back as 200 B.C., Chinese emperors had teams of servants search the country for all kinds of art. The ever-growing collection was kept at the emperor's palace in Beijing. The revolution of 1911 ended imperial rule in China, and the KMT gained control of the country and the art collection. During the civil war between the Communists and the Nationalists, Chiang Kai-shek had the collection moved from one stronghold to another. In 1949, after the Communists won the civil war, the KMT moved it again, this time to Taipei.

The collection remained in warehouses until 1965, when the National Palace Museum opened. The collection contains an estimated 650,000 pieces, so only a small part of it is on display at any one time.

artists began seeking inspiration and subjects in Taiwan's folk traditions. This "Taiwan Consciousness" movement gained momentum after 1970.

Chinese Ceramics

China's long history of ceramics goes back some eight thousand years. The most famous ceramics, developed more than five hundred years ago, were blue and white porcelain. By 1800, this porcelain was prized throughout the world and became known as Chinaware.

Artists in Taiwan have carried on the Chinese ceramics tradition. The town of Yingge in northern Taiwan houses the world-famous Yingge Ceramics Museum, and the streets are lined with more than one hundred pottery shops and factories.

In the 1980s, the opening of the Taipei Fine Arts Museum helped make the international art world aware of Taiwan's artistic achievements. Since then, Taiwanese artists have become even more intent on creating the island's own art history. Artists such as Yuan Goang-ming and Chen Chieh-jen have gained international recognition for their examination of the emptiness and loneliness of modern cities like Taipei.

Performing Arts

There are two forms of opera in Taiwan: Beijing opera and Taiwanese opera. Both are striking and, for Westerners, quite unusual. Beijing opera originated about a thousand years ago. To some Westerners, it is a jumble of unfamiliar sounds, including shrill voices, banging gongs, loud drums, screeching wind instruments, and string instruments that sometimes sound like fingernails on a chalkboard. Beijing opera is also, as one reviewer noted, "a visual feast." It has brightly colored costumes and lots of exciting action, including acrobatics and martial arts.

Chinese opera was introduced to Taiwan in the seventeenth century and slowly evolved into something separate. At first, Taiwanese opera was only performed on special occasions, like weddings or festivals. Then it became more public, with performances in parks and marketplaces. Taiwanese opera mixes elements of Beijing opera with folk songs and aboriginal music. The instruments are also somewhat different.

The action in both Beijing and Taiwanese opera is largely symbolic. A flick of the sleeve registers disgust, or rubbing hands together means worry. A chair placed on a table becomes a mountain, but if a person is sitting in that chair, it is a throne. Costumes and makeup are also symbolic. Red means loyalty or honesty, while white represents cunning or evil. The emperor wears yellow, and a student is usually in blue.

An opera performer in Taipei. Chinese opera usually involves ornate costumes and makeup.

The Cloud Gate Dance Company

Modern dance has been popular in Taiwan since the 1940s, when it was introduced by the Japanese. Taiwan's most famous dance company, the Cloud Gate, was formed in the 1970s by Lin Hwai-min, who had been a student of Martha Graham, the famous American dancer and choreographer. Like other Taiwanese groups, the Cloud Gate Dance Company combines modern dance with elements of Chinese opera and aboriginal folk dances.

In the company's early years, dances were based on stories and legends from classical Chinese literature. The company then began exploring issues of Taiwan's identity. *Legacy*, for example, tells the story of Taiwan's early settlers. The creative mix of the island's artists is reflected in Lin's work entitled *Nine Songs*. In this dance, he set the verses of the ancient Chinese poet Chu Yuan to movements borrowed from Beijing opera and to dance borrowed from India and Indonesia. The beautiful color and movements were a great hit when *Nine Songs* was performed in New York City in 1995.

Music

The Taiwanese love of music ranges from traditional orchestral music to modern pop and alternative sounds. Traditional Chinese music is often based on ancient Chinese poetry. Unlike Western music, in Chinese music melody is less important than tone. The music is played by classical orchestras on instruments that include two- and three-stringed mandolins, zithers, flutes, and two-stringed violas.

For many years, popular music in Taiwan was made up mostly of overly sweet love songs. Since the 1990s, a livelier music scene has emerged from outdoor music festivals that began with an event called the Ragged Live Festival in Taipei in 1994. The next year, the Spring Scream, a musical event held at Kending, was very successful. It has been held every year since.

Taiwanese singer Jonathan Lee performs in Shanghai, China, in 2005. Lee is also one of Taiwan's top popular music producers.

Taiwanese popular music itself is generally labeled "Mando pop" because the lyrics are sung in Mandarin. Lyrics are simple, usually dealing with the love that was, or that is going to be, or that can never be. The clean-cut performers are usually also popular in Hong Kong and other parts of Southeast Asia.

Aboriginal Arts and Crafts

Each indigenous tribe in Taiwan has developed its own forms of arts and crafts. Works from nine different aboriginal groups are on display at the Shung Ye Museum of Formosan Aborigines in Taipei. The exhibits show what the various tribes have in common, as well as what makes them unique.

Several of the tribes are known for their wood carving. The Yami of Lanyu Island, for example, make fantastic canoes, with carved designs painted red, black, and white. Each canoe is constructed out of twenty-seven separate pieces using no nails or glue. The Paiwan and Rukai are also outstanding wood-carvers. Their homes feature imaginative carvings of humans, animals, and legendary creatures. The Atayal are famous for their weaving. They produce elaborate designs in contrasting colors.

The ongoing search for a Taiwanese identity has contributed to great interest in preserving and promoting the arts of the indigenous people. This is particularly true of music and dance. Several tribes have used vocal music as a way to preserve their heritage, and these

Woodcarving has become more popular in recent years. These older carvings can be seen at the Taiwan Handicraft Centre in Taipei.

Puppets in All Sizes

Puppet shows have been popular in Taiwan for at least two hundred years. They are often part of religious festivals. The puppets are usually shown driving out evil spirits or thanking the gods. The puppets in religious festivals are marionettes, large puppets moved by strings. Another type of puppet used in Taiwan is shadow puppets. These are slightly smaller than marionettes. They are moved behind a screen so that only the shadow is seen. In glove puppetry, the puppets fit over the hand. They are made with colorful and detailed clothing, and their actions, including dances and martial arts, require extraordinary skill.

folk songs are now popular throughout Taiwan. Aboriginal dance is also popular and growing more so every year. Most of the dances were developed for particular purposes, but a large part of their value today seems to be to entertain busloads of tourists. One of the most popular dance groups in Taiwan is the Formosa Aboriginal Dance Troupe. It includes dancers from several tribes and has performed internationally.

Film

The Japanese introduced filmmaking to Taiwan in the early 1900s. Under the Nationalists, the government was mainly interested in films that promoted the official government viewpoint. By the 1960s, Taiwanese directors were making some good films, but few people went to see them. They preferred the big hits from Hong Kong and the United States.

Ang Lee won a Golden Globe award in 2001 for Best Director for his film *Crouching Tiger, Hidden Dragon.* Lee now makes most of his films in the United States.

In the past twenty years, Taiwanese film has come into its own. Director Hou Hsiao-hsien led what was called the New Wave movement. His film *The Sandwich Man* (1983) was one of the first Taiwanese movies to examine the tough realities of city life. Ang Lee is Taiwan's most famous and successful filmmaker. He has also been one of the most courageous. In 1993, his film *The Wedding Banquet* caused controversy for its treatment of homosexuality. Ang Lee has gone on to achieve great success with American films like *Sense and Sensibility* (1995) and *The Ice Storm* (1997). In 2000, he gained worldwide fame for his martial arts film *Crouching Tiger, Hidden Dragon*, which won four Academy Awards. Despite such successes, the Taiwanese film industry still has not yet won a wide following among the island's population.

Literature

Although Taiwanese writers have produced many novels and short-story collections, little of their work is known outside Taiwan. The main reason for this seems to be that few books by Taiwanese authors have been translated into English.

Cinema Pioneer

In the early 1980s, film director Hou Hsiao-hsien decided he had to do something to change the direction of the Taiwanese film industry. The island's filmmakers had been producing cheap films filled with sex and violence and calling them social realism. Hou Hsiao-hsien decided that his films really would present social realism. They would examine the conflicts involved in Taiwan's rapid change from a rural country to a fast-paced urban society.

His first great success came in 1983 with *The Sandwich Man*, which was based on three short stories by the author Huang Chun-ming. One of the stories, "The Taste of Bitter Apples," concerns a young boy who moves from a rural village to Taipei, with tragic results. This film is considered the first of a "new wave" of Taiwanese cinema, which has become popular in the cities of Europe and North America.

Hou Hsaio-hsien gained even greater international fame with *City of Sadness*. In this 1989 film, he offers a stark portrayal of the KMT takeover of Taiwan.

It earned one of film's top prizes, the Golden Lion award at the Venice Film Festival. Hou has continued to produce outstanding motion pictures, including *The Puppet Master* and *Millennium Mambo*.

In the modern quest for a Taiwanese identity, many writers have focused on the difficult adjustment to city life. They explore issues like drug use and urban decay. Books with a broader view of social issues have become increasingly popular and widely praised outside Taiwan. Huang Chun-ming's *A Taste of Bitter Apples* is considered a modern classic. Li Qiao's highly acclaimed *Wintry Night* tells the fifty-year story of one family of Chinese settlers in Taiwan.

Food, Festivals, and Everyday Life

ONE OF THE MOST STRIKING FEATURES OF LIFE IN TAIWAN is the remarkable friendliness of the people. Stop a stranger on a crowded Taipei street to ask for directions and that person is likely to simply take you where you want to go. You may even be asked to join their family for dinner. Visit Taiwan and you'll quickly discover a people with a joyful, energetic approach to life.

Opposite: **A man wears traditional face paint at the Lantern Festival.**

Many Food Choices

Food in Taiwan reflects the island's history. Each new immigrant group has brought its own cuisine, and the Taiwanese

People eating at a night market in Taipei. Eating out is a popular pastime for the Taiwanese.

have welcomed foods from Europe, other Asian countries, and the United States. The result is choices and more choices, and the Taiwanese take great pleasure in trying to sample them all. Eating out is popular with people of all ages, and the evening scene in restaurants is lively and noisy. People enjoy foods in all kinds of places, from snack food stalls to fancy restaurants.

There are several styles of cooking in Taiwan, in both homes and restaurants. Most styles are based on the regional cooking of mainland China. Here is a brief rundown of the major cuisines.

Taiwanese

There is no widespread agreement on what Taiwanese food is. In general, it is based on aboriginal foods, with an emphasis on seafood, sweet potatoes, and taro root. A traditional Taiwanese breakfast includes watery rice and seaweed, with baked or steamed buns and hot soy milk. Recently, Western breakfasts such as fried eggs and coffee have become popular. Lunch is usually between noon and two o'clock. Most people eat lunch at cafeterias or fast-food restaurants. Dinner, whether eaten at home or in restaurants, usually comes from one of the mainland China cuisines.

The people of Taiwan have a huge array of food to choose from.

Cantonese

Cantonese food, from the southern Chinese province of Guandong, is what Americans often think of as "Chinese." Fresh ingredients, such as snow peas or broccoli, are important, as are the texture and appearance of the food. Sweet and sour sauces are common. Specialties include abalone, shark's fin, and bird's nest soups. Snacks such as spring rolls or dumplings are popular. Common steamed or stir-fried foods include chicken or beef with oyster sauce. Rice is the staple side dish.

Beijing

This cooking style is from northern China. Wheat replaces rice as the staple. The wheat is used for an array of noodles, dumplings, and buns stuffed with meat, vegetables, or both. The most famous Beijing dish is Peking duck, which is often served at banquets.

Dumplings are popular in Taiwan. They are often filled with pork, crab, or shrimp.

Shanghainese

Coming from the central coastal region of China, this cuisine offers a variety of seafood as well as poultry. The food tends to be a little sweeter than Cantonese and is oily. Popular dishes include drunken chicken (chicken marinated in wine sauce) and steamed crab. Either rice or wheat-based noodles and buns are common.

Sichuanese

The southwestern province of Sichuan is known for having the spiciest of all Chinese foods. Chili peppers, as well as peppercorns and other seasonings, can be deadly hot if you're not used to them. Milder dishes are also available. Beef, pork, and chicken are used, but seafood is not.

Tea Drinking

Tea drinking is a national pastime in Taiwan. It has been practiced for more than a thousand years, and today it is considered a necessity of life. Tea is drunk at stands and in shops. Groups of elderly men are often seen on the streets, gathered together around a teapot. People also enjoy visiting the many teahouses tucked into the mountains.

Throughout Taiwan there are regional tea-tasting competitions, where tea farmers, sellers, and experts compete. When a tea is judged to be good, it becomes popular and its price increases.

Tea farms abound in Taiwan. Tea leaves grow on trees and are picked while they are young and tender. The leaves are brewed in small, decorative pots and served in clear cups so the color can be seen. In Taiwan, tea drinking is thought to be good for people's health. The Taiwanese believe tea improves eyesight and alertness.

New Drinks

Tea is the basic beverage in Taiwan, as it is in China. Besides the basic teas, a drink called bubble tea has become popular in recent years. Today, there are bubble tea stands on every other street corner. Bubble tea is a mixture of tea, flavoring, sugar, and large tapioca balls. Passion fruit or papaya are the usual flavorings. Chewy tapioca at the bottom of the cup is sipped through large straws.

Chinese Noodles

One of the favorite foods at Taiwanese festivals and celebrations is noodles. Noodles were likely first made in northern China in around 220 B.C. They became popular because they were cheap, nutritious, portable, and easily stored. According to legend, an Italian named Marco Polo brought the first noodles to Italy in 1295 after his travels in China.

Several types of noodles are popular in Taiwan. Hand-pulled noodles are made by repeatedly stretching wheat flour dough. Thin rice flour noodles are also common. To the Taiwanese, the long, thin shape of noodles symbolizes a long life. That is why it is bad luck to break them before cooking.

A fruit market in Taitung. Many Taiwanese enjoy fruit smoothies made from the wide variety of fruit that grows in Taiwan.

Stands selling juices and fruit smoothies are increasingly popular in Taiwan, especially in hot weather. Coffee, which was introduced by the Japanese, was only mildly popular until the 1990s when American coffee shops like Starbucks invaded the island. Coffee now rivals tea in popularity, at least among younger Taiwanese.

Snacks and Fast Foods

Taiwan's lively and colorful night markets are famous for good food at modest prices. A kind of Taiwanese ravioli is popular, as are such street snacks as fried tofu, baked sweet potatoes, and tea eggs soaked in soy sauce. Most Americans avoid Taiwanese specialties like chickens' feet or

The Dos and Don'ts of Eating in Taiwan

While waiting for your food, don't play with your chopsticks, and never stick them in the rice bowl because vertical chopsticks symbolize death.

It's okay to hold a bowl of rice or thick soup close to your mouth and shovel the food with your chopsticks.

Always serve your companions tea before pouring your own.

When someone pours tea for you, thank the pourer by gently tapping on the table with your middle finger.

When you need a fresh pot of tea, simply remove the lid and set it on the table.

Don't poke around in the communal bowl for the tasty pieces of food.

Never serve food from the communal bowl using your chopsticks.

pigs' ears. The Taiwanese also enjoy a variety of European and American fast foods, including hamburgers, Belgian waffles, pizza, and tacos.

Festivals

Throughout the year, the Taiwanese celebrate festivals with great gusto. The festivals are colorful and cheerful, often including fireworks, parades, puppet shows, and good food. Many have their origins in folk religion, Taoism, and Buddhism. Some holidays in Taiwan follow the lunar calendar, so they fall at different times each year, while others follow the Western calendar.

A Calendar of Festivals and Holidays

Founding Day	January 1
Chinese New Year	January or February
2-28	February 28
Tomb Sweep Day	April 5
Birth of Matsu	April or May
Dragon Boat Festival	June
Teachers' Day	September 28
Moon Festival	September or October
National Day	October 10
Retrocession Day	October 25
Constitution Day	December 25

Lion dancers are part of the celebration on National Day. The lion dance is supposed to bring good luck and happiness.

The most important Taiwanese holiday is Chinese New Year, which begins on the first day of the first lunar month. The celebration officially goes on until the fifth day of the month, but by tradition it continues all the way until the fifteenth. Chinese New Year is the time to get rid of everything old and bring in the new by cleaning house, buying new clothes, and paying off debts. People send gifts of money in red envelopes.

Chinese New Year is Taiwan's biggest festival. Each year, a giant party is held at the Taipei city hall.

The Lantern Festival on the fifteenth of the first month ends Chinese New Year. This is the island's most colorful festival, with fireworks and countless lanterns. Small lanterns are handed out to the crowds of people, while thousands of larger lanterns are launched into the night sky around Pingxi. The festivities can last up to five days.

Two huge lanterns in the shape of sheep horns light up Taipei during the Lantern Festival. The origins of the Lantern Festival may date back two thousand years.

Taiwan's Calendar

The Taiwanese have their own calendar system, though they also use the Western system and the Chinese system. The Taiwanese have had a special system since 1911, the year the Republic of China was founded.

In Taiwan, the Western year 1911 is the year 0. That makes 2005 the year 94 in the Taiwanese system. The date June 30, 2005, would be written 94/06/30 (94 for the year, 06 for the month, and 30 for the day).

Sports

Organized sports were not important in Taiwan until the five-day workweek was instituted a few years ago. With more leisure time, people became more interested in recreational sports like hiking, biking, and jogging. In the past decade, the government has been building new parks and sports centers. Schools now require physical education at all age levels. Students learn martial arts as well as baseball or softball, volleyball, and soccer.

Martial arts such as tai chi are popular in Taiwan. Tai chi improves strength, balance, and flexibility, and also reduces stress.

Basketball and baseball are both popular sports in Taiwan. Basketball has become popular recently, partly because it can be played both indoors and outdoors and because it requires little equipment. Baseball has been even more popular, especially Little League. Professional baseball has sometimes struggled in Taiwan. In 2003, the island's two professional leagues merged into one. The league includes such teams as the Brother Elephants, the China Trust Whales, and the President Lions. None of the teams has a home stadium, so games are played in different cities.

Taiwan's national baseball team celebrates a victory over China in the Asian Championships. In 2002, Chin-Feng Chen became the first Taiwanese to play Major League Baseball in the United States.

Martial arts have long been important to the Taiwanese. They see martial arts as a way to stay fit and regulate a person's *chi* or "vital energy." Of the more than twenty martial arts, tai chi is the most popular. At dawn every day, people gather in parks all over the island to practice this slow-motion activity that looks like shadow boxing.

Living with Change

The great friendliness of the Taiwanese people—they call it being *haoke* ("good hosts")—is deeply ingrained. It is one of the traditions they rely on to help them deal with the rapid changes of modern society. The Taiwanese try hard to create harmony and balance in their lives in everything from the arrangement of objects on a desk to getting along with others.

Family members rely on each other in Taiwan. More than half of elderly people live with their married children.

The concept of "face" is another tradition that promotes harmony and a feeling of security. It simply means avoiding behavior that would embarrass another person. Losing one's temper in public would be a way of losing face.

Another important tradition is the idea of *guanxi*. This is a tight network of family and friends who help one another, especially when someone has a problem. People often solve

Some Dos and Don'ts

Always take your shoes off when entering a Taiwanese home.

Don't give a handkerchief as a gift because it means you think the person will soon cry.

Don't write in red ink, unless you're writing a letter of protest or correcting an exam.

When entering a room, always greet the eldest person first as a sign of respect.

problems by asking a friend or a relative for help, rather than relying on other channels, such as a government bureaucracy. Once a favor is granted, the person who received the favor is under obligation to return it in some way. Thus, guanxi becomes one more way of maintaining harmony.

The most important tradition that guides Taiwanese life is relying on the family. Most Taiwanese live in crowded cities, often with five or six people in an apartment with three tiny bedrooms. People sometimes find creative ways to add a room on a flat roof or out into a side alley. But more than anything else, they depend on close family ties to avoid the stress of crowded conditions.

Rapid change has brought both benefits and problems to the people of Taiwan. On the plus side, the Taiwanese have created one of the highest living standards in the world. Change has also meant more educational and career opportunities.

On the negative side, change has caused pollution, a housing shortage, and social problems like more crime and drug use. The government has not been able to ensure the safety of food and water supplies. The Taiwanese are well aware of these problems, but they do not seem weighed down by them. The combination of a high standard of living and the strength of their traditions gives them an optimistic outlook about the present and the future.

Taiwan is a prosperous country with a good school system. This gives the Taiwanese great hope for the future.

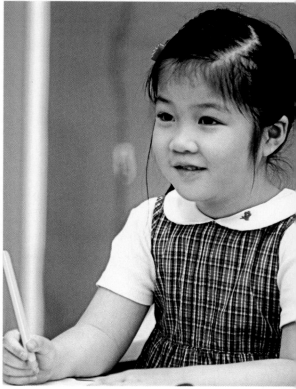

Timeline

Taiwanese History		World History	
People from the Pacific islands and Southeast Asia inhabit Taiwan.	10,000 B.C.		
		2500 B.C.	Egyptians build the Pyramids and the Sphinx in Giza.
		563 B.C.	The Buddha is born in India.
		A.D. 313	The Roman emperor Constantine recognizes Christianity.
		610	The Prophet Muhammad begins preaching a new religion called Islam.
		1054	The Eastern (Orthodox) and Western (Roman) Churches break apart.
		1066	William the Conqueror defeats the English in the Battle of Hastings.
		1095	Pope Urban II proclaims the First Crusade.
		1215	King John seals the Magna Carta.
		1300s	The Renaissance begins in Italy.
		1347	The Black Death sweeps through Europe.
Large numbers of settlers arrive from China.	A.D. 1400s	1453	Ottoman Turks capture Constantinople, conquering the Byzantine Empire.
		1492	Columbus arrives in North America.
Portuguese sailors become the first Europeans in Taiwan.	1590	1500s	The Reformation leads to the birth of Protestantism.
The Dutch take control of the Penghu Islands.	1622		
The Spanish take over the northern portion of the island.	1626		
The Dutch regain control of all of Taiwan.	1642		
The Ming drive the Dutch from Taiwan.	1661		
Tainan is the capital of Taiwan.	1663–1885	1776	The Declaration of Independence is signed.
		1789	The French Revolution begins.

Taiwanese History

Taiwan is given to Japan as a result of the Sino-Japanese War.	1895
Japan loses World War II and gives Taiwan back to China.	1945
The Nationalist Chinese government escapes to Taiwan.	1949
Mainland China bombards Kinmen Island with artillery.	1958
The Republic of China loses its seat in the United Nations.	1971
Chiang Kai-shek dies.	1975
Martial law is lifted.	1987
The National Assembly elects Lee Teng-shui president.	1988
Lee Teng-shui is reelected in Taiwan's first democratic election.	1996
Fifty-five years of Nationalist Party rule ends with the election of Chen Shui-bian.	2000
Five typhoons hit Taiwan.	2001

World History

1865	The American Civil War ends.
1914	World War I breaks out.
1917	The Bolshevik Revolution brings communism to Russia.
1929	Worldwide economic depression begins.
1939	World War II begins, following the German invasion of Poland.
1945	World War II ends.
1957	The Vietnam War starts.
1969	Humans land on the moon.
1975	The Vietnam War ends.
1979	Soviet Union invades Afghanistan.
1983	Drought and famine in Africa.
1989	The Berlin Wall is torn down, as communism crumbles in Eastern Europe.
1991	Soviet Union breaks into separate states.
1992	Bill Clinton is elected U.S. president.
2000	George W. Bush is elected U.S. president.
2001	Terrorists attack World Trade Towers, New York, and the Pentagon, Washington, D.C.
2003	The U.S. invades Iraq.

Fast Facts

Official name: Republic of China (conventional long form)

Taiwan (conventional short form)

Capital: Taipei

Official language: Mandarin Chinese

Taipei

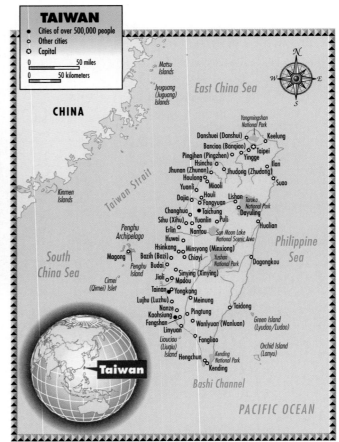

Taiwan's flag

Year of founding:	1912
National anthem:	"San Min Chu I" ("The Rights of the People")
Government:	Multiparty democracy
Chief of state:	President
Head of government:	Premier
Area:	14,015 square miles (36,300 sq km)
Bordering countries:	None
Highest elevation:	Yushan (Jade Mountain), 12,966 feet (3,952 m)
Lowest elevation:	Sea level
Average July temperature:	86°F (30°C)
Average January temperature:	65°F (18°C)
Average annual precipitation:	99 inches (252 cm)
National population (July 2005 est.):	22,894,384

Population of major cities:

Taipei	2,706,400
Kaohsiung	1,506,300
Taichung	1,033,600
Tainan	746,300

Bamboo forest

Taroko Gorge

The new Taiwan dollar

Famous landmarks: ▶ *Taipei Fine Arts Museum*, Taipei

▶ *Chiang Kai-shek Memorial*, Taipei

▶ *National Palace Museum*, Taipei

▶ *Sun Moon Lake*, Nantou County

▶ *Taroko Gorge*, Hualien

▶ *Ami Culture Village*, Hualien

Industry: Taiwan has a strong economy with many high-tech firms and research institutes. It exports much more than it imports. Its leading products include computers, digital cameras, computer software, and electrical components. Agriculture makes up less than 2 percent of the economy.

Currency: The Taiwan dollar. As of September 2005, one U.S. dollar was worth 32.44 Taiwan dollars.

System of weights and measures: Metric system

Literacy rate: 96.1 percent

Common words and phrases in Mandarin:

Ni hao	Where is . . . ?
Zaijian	Goodbye
Qing	Please
Xiexie	Thank you
Duoxie	Many thanks
Nin guixing?	What is your name?
Wo xing . . .	My surname is . . .

Taiwanese student

Ang Lee

Famous Taiwanese:

Chen Shui-bian *President of Taiwan*	(1950–)	
Chiang Kai-shek *First president of the* *Republic of China*	(1887–1975)	
Hou Hsiao-hsien *Filmmaker*	(1947–)	
Ang Lee *Filmmaker*	(1954–)	
Lee Teng-hui *President from 1988 to 2000*	(1923–)	
Lin Hwai-min *Dancer*	(1947–)	
Huang Chun-ming *Novelist*	(1939–)	
Annette Lu *Political leader imprisoned* *for promoting democracy and* *who is now vice president*	(1944–)	

To Find Out More

Books

▶ Green, Robert. *Taiwan*. San Diego: Greenhaven Press, 2004.

▶ Ryan, Michaela. *Taiwan*. Milwaukee, WI: Gareth Stevens Publishing, 2003.

▶ Salter, Christopher. *Taiwan*. Philadelphia: Chelsea House, 2004.

▶ Wan, Vanessa. *Welcome to Taiwan*. Milwaukee, WI: Gareth Stevens Publishing, 2004.

▶ Wee, Jessie. *Taiwan*. Philadelphia: Chelsea House, 1998.

Web Sites

▶ **Frontline: Dangerous Straits**
http://www.pbs.org/wgbh/pages/
frontline/shows/china/
A PBS site on China-Taiwan relations.

▶ **Taiwan Government
Information Office**
http://www.gio.gov.tw/
*For all kinds of information, including
history, current news, and travel tips.*

▶ **The World Factbook on Taiwan**
http://www.cia.gov/cia/publications/
factbook/geos/tw.html
*For information about the government,
economy, people, and geography
of Taiwan.*

Organizations

▶ **Taipei Economic and
Cultural Office**
555 Montgomery Street
San Francisco, CA 94111
(415) 989-8677

Index

Page numbers in *italics* indicate illustrations.

Meet the Author

DAVID C. KING is a full-time freelance writer. He has written more than sixty books for children and young adults, including a dozen books about other cultures. His multimedia program titled *Perception/Misperception, China/USA*, won several awards.

Although he usually writes American history and biography, King also enjoys writing about other countries. "Writing means learning—all the time," King says. "You also discover that culture is a mirror that offers you new perspectives on your own society." Can you write about another country without visiting it? King points out that anthropologist Ruth Benedict wrote her classic study of Japanese culture, *The Chrysanthemum and the Sword*, without visiting Japan. "The important thing," King believes, "is the author's sensitivity to the people and their way of life, along with careful and thorough research." It also helps to talk with citizens of the country. King's understanding of life in Taiwan has been helped by friendship with the family of a former officer in the Taiwanese air force.

King is a former editor with the Foreign Policy Association. He has written for the World Bank, UNICEF, and UNESCO, and has been a consultant to the U.S. Department of Education and several state departments of education. His wife, Sharon, often shares research and writing assignments, and they coauthored an award-winning book on the Statue of Liberty. Their home in the Berkshires at the junction of New York, Connecticut, and Massachusetts is a great jumping-off point for their travels.

Photo Credits